OLD CITY

OLD BEIJING
In the Shadow of Imperial Throne
Text by Xu Chengbei

Text by: Xu Chengbei
Photos by: China Photo Archive
China No.2 Historical Archive
Translatad by: Wang Mingjie
English text edited by: Foster Stockwell
Edited by: Sun Shuming

First edition 2001

**Old Beijing
— In the Shadow of Imperial Throne**

ISBN 7-119-02786-7

© Foreign Languages Press
Published by Foreign Languages Press
24 Baiwanzhuang Road, Beijing 100037, China
Home Page:http://www.flp.com.cn
E-mail Addresses: info@flp.com.cn
　　　　　　　　sales@flp.com.cn
Printed in the People's Republic of China

Foreword

In the past my books have been published only in text form. Occasionally I have used a few photos for supplementary purposes. But, at the request of the Jiangsu Art Publishing House, I have recently completed this book, *Old Beijing*, which contains both text and pictures. The commissioning editor of the publishing house told me that the theme and style would have no limits set by them. So I decided that the book should be composed of three parts. The first part would be written in chronological order. It would be a history of Beijing from the "Ji" period of three thousand years before to the late Qing dynasty (1644-1911) and the early Republic of China (1911-1949) in the early 20th century. The second part would be a description of life in Beijing during the late Qing and early Republic period. And the third part would concentrate on the characteristics of Beijing and its people in the past. After hearing these ideas, the commissioning editor, while praising them as "rather ambitious", expressed his concern that it would be impossible to get any good photos to illustrate the first part.

Without much thinking, I wrote the first part in one stretch. But when I reread it, my own brows began to knit. Where on earth can we find photos for the Liao, Jin, Yuan and Ming dynasties, not to say the period of Ji? Before the publishing house made any further comments, I gave this direction up. I had to start all over again. For a couple of days, I took pains to work out a new plan, but that would not do; then another, but that would not work either. I had never had such experiences in writing in the past. Helpless, I faced my bookcases and began scanning books. Suddenly my eyes fell on a book entitled *Is This Beijing?*, compiled by Jiang Mingde. It is a collection of articles about the city written by some elderly literati residing in Beijing. The articles were published between 1919 to 1949.

I opened the book and began to read the Editor's Note. Mr. Jiang described what he had seen when he first entered Beijing: "The train drove straight into the Qianmen Gate Railway Station. When I got off, I looked up at Jian Lou (Arrow Tower) for quite some time. Then I had a bowl of bean curd at a little food stall. Suddenly several little beggars, dressed in tatters, came up to me, stretching out their hands for help." Great! My book could start by following Mr. Jiang into Beijing. Among several hundred photos collected by the publishing house from many sources, I was able to find a photo of the Arrow Tower in a sleet storm. The photo had been taken from an upward angle. Nearby there was a food stall with an awning over it. Perfect! It was just my day.

In recent years, I have made a study of both Peking opera and well-known commercial establishments, and from this, my interest has grown to all aspects of local culture in Beijing. I have published more than thirty books about this subject. As for this particular book, my first plan for it was not realizable. It was the format that included a combination of both words and pictures that forced me to blaze a new trail. I have also come to recognize that pictures and words supplement each other in a publication, and that is why books of this sort are so popular today. Readers love the smooth and easy reading of such books. As life rhythm quickens, many persons have no time for profound reading. This poses a new challenge to both writers and their literary works. It hampers writers from going into the depths of their subject, not to mention the fact that it does not allow them to let out all that is in their minds.

Shortly after completing the book, the editor posted the galley proofs to me. When I read them, I was pleasantly surprised to find that the book had become more interesting after the commissioning editor added "branches and leaves" through illustrations. Though a book with illustrations might limit a writer to a certain extent, you must admit that it becomes more readable. No wonder the commissioning editor assured me that this book would arouse great interest among publishers and the reading public. Perhaps they have both a theoretical and a practical basis. I, too, wish them success.

Xu Chengbei
Beijing, September 1998

CONTENTS

Foreword Xu Chengbei
Chapter 1 Entering Beijing
(3) An Old City Covered with the Dust of Ages
(13) Surviving Towers

Chapter 2 Capital of the Empire
The Eternal Axis(23)
A Symmetrical Imperial City(31)
"Traces" Left by the "Sons of Heaven"(37)
Overlooking Central China(41)
"Imperial Air" Must not Be Leaked out(53)

Chapter 3 The Fall of the Dynasty
(63) Yuan Ming Yuan in Its Last Days
(71) The Qing Emperor Learned A New word: "Concession"

Chapter 4 streets and Alleys
Old Archways in Photos(81)
Hutongs(85)
Step by Step, Just No Hurry(95)

Chapter 5 Morning Bell and Evening Drum
(107)Wordless Sound
(117)Religion, A Walking-stick for the Ruler
(121)Coexistence of Buddhism, Taoism and Confucianism
(127)Women of Gentle Character and Men with A Sense of Justice

Chapter 6 Temple Fairs and Theaters
Childhood Dreams(135)
Theatre, Opera Stars and Fans(149)
Lamentation(159)

Chapter 7 Subordinates of the Capital
(167)Minced Sheep Offal and Salty Pepper
(175)Clothes, Food, Housing and Traffic
(195)Beijingers of the Past Seen in Photos

Chapter 8 A Picture of Secular Life
A Place of Significant Events(209)
Three Festivals in the Capital(221)
Awning, Fish Pot and Pomegranates,Chef,
Fat Dog and Plump Girl(231)

Chapter 1
Entering Beijing

Silhouette of the ancient city in mist.

An Old City Covered with the Dust of Ages

"I still remember my first impression of Beijing when I first visited the city. As the train entered Dongbian Gate, the windows brushed past the wall of the city. The aged, solid bricks were covered with the dust of ages. The top of the wall was strewn with weeds. It was indeed a picture of dereliction and deterioration. However, the site still aroused my longing and great respect for this ancient city. This was not because I later visited the awe-inspiring Imperial Palace, but it was because of the pride I had for the city's history, and for the nation and its culture.

"As soon as I emerged from the Qianmen Railway Station, I was stunned by the magnificence of the Qianmen Gate Tower and the Arrow Tower. I felt that I was quite small standing at the foot of them. Yes, I was turning twenty in age at that time, and truly gazed at them in amazement. I gaped at so many towers and such a long city wall. It was a metropolitan city which was familiar yet strange to me.

"At the foot of the Arrow Tower, there were many food stalls. I found a bean curd stall that appeared slightly cleaner than most of the others and sat down on a little stool. As I held up a bowl of bean curd, there came five or six small beggars from god knows where, stretching their dirty hands towards me. Even today I still remember the tatters they were covered with and their waxy faces and hungry expressions. Is this our capital? Are these citizens of the capital?"
　　　　— Jiang Deming: "Foreword" from *Is This Beijing?*

This is writer Jiang Deming's impression when he first visited Beijing. At that time, this city was named Beiping. A few years ago, Mr. Jiang, as the chief compiler, published *Is This Beijing?*. It is a collection of 121 articles about the city written by 74 contemporary writers. They vividly and minutely describe historical events that took place in Beijing over a span of thirty years from 1919 to 1949.

Mr. Jiang entered Beijing by train and arrived at Qianmen, the center of the city, immediately. Before 1959, the Beijing Railway Station was located in Qianmen. The proper name of Qianmen Gate is Zhengyang Gate, the southern entrance to the inner city of Beijing.

Zhengyang Gate and its Arrow Tower.

Snow in old Beijing. Sadness fills this true street scene.

The first train entered Beijing by running through an opening in the city wall.

Beijing first became the capital during the Liao dynasty and remained so through the Jin (1115-1234), Yuan (1206-1368), Ming (1368-1644) and Qing (1644-1911) dynasties. Before that, it was never a capital and there was no such name as Beijing. The reason China has its size of today has a lot to do with the functions of Beijing. Beijing is located in the north of Central China, to the south of the Northeast inhabited by many ethnic peoples. It experiences simultaneously the existence of the powers as well as attractions from both sides. At the same time it exercises its influence on both sides. Let's suppose, if there had not been Beijing or Beijing had not been a capital, Central China would have remained Central China and Northeast would have remained the Northeast. In other words, Central China would have been occupied respectively by some warlords, while the Northeast would have had endless wars. That being the case, there would not have

Rickshaw boys wait for customers in the wind and snow at the foot of Zhengyang Gate.

been the birth of a large, prosperous and united China. Fortunately, since the Liao dynasty (907-1125) the power forces of the Northeast ruled Beijing for a period of time. But before long, the power forces of Central China returned to Beijing and gradually grew stronger and prosperous. Later on the power forces of the Northeast became more powerful again and Beijing ruled the country at the will of the Northeast. After a few rounds of such a tug of war, Beijing finally became a combination of the two power forces. It has emerged as the only center that possesses the cohesive and ruling control over all China. During the Yuan, Ming and Qing dynasties and later during the Republic of China (191-1949), Beijing

The imperial seal of Emperor Zheng De of the Ming dynasty became part of the collection owned by Emperor Guang Xu (ruled from 1875 to 1908).

The Great Wall, witness to many important historical events in China.

showed its most significant function both in military and political affairs.

Beijing is situated in an area with a scarcity of resources. The mountains are not high; the waters are not deep. Since it was where the imperial house was located, the main topics of conversation of this city were maintaining rule and attempting to overthrow the existing power. The minority lived on the activities of the majority. People living in the inner city relied on those living outside. Often this was not adequate. So grain, building materials, and even craftsmen had to be supplied from outside Beijing. Beijing was a typical consumer city, relying on various provinces, ethnic kingdoms and foreign contributors to keep it going.

The history of China was a history of changing dynasties. Even the clothing worn by the statues of generals and ministers guarding the imperial mausoleums kept changing.

The imperial seal of Emperor Jia Qing (ruled from 1522 to 1566) was in a collectionowned by a Qing emperor.

This is a photo of the seventeen-arch bridge in the Summer Palace taken some sixty years ago. The girl standing by the balustrade must be over eighty now.

This, the capital, should have more people with laughter and joy and less people in tatters and with waxen faces.

A caravan of camels loaded with contributory gifts for the imperial house.

Surviving Towers

The rostrum of Zhengyang Gate, the most magnificent structure of the city gates in Beijing. Beijingers in the past called it the Qianmen Lou (tower). It was renovated in 1915. The blockhouse outside the city was pulled down and a square was built.

Before railways were built in Beijing, the entrance gates to the city were closely watched. Any outsiders entering Beijing had to follow stipulated routes. Merchants from the south could either come on a dusty road leading to the Yongding Gate of the outer city or sail along the Grand Canal to Tongzhou, then enter the Tonghui River to reach the customs at the Chongwen Gate before finally arriving at Jishuitan in the northwest part of the inner city. Travelers from the north had to go through the Juyong Pass of the Great Wall, reach Nankou and then enter the city by the Desheng Gate. Because of its auspicious name, troops going out on military expeditions always passed through the Desheng (virtue and victory) Gate. When troops went out or returned, ordinary people had to keep away from the Gate.

In the olden days, Beijing had twenty-odd city gates, each having its own function. Xizhi Gate, for instance, located in the northwest, was a passage for

This is the Jianruiying Martial Art Practicing Hall at the foot of the Fragrant Hill. Manchurians established the Qing dynasty through their military strength. When they became rulers of China, they did not neglect the practice of martial arts.

Clouds of dust and the clinking of camels' bells on a windy autumn day. This was a scene of old Beijing.

The Arrow Tower of Xuanwu Gate. When criminals were taken to Caishikou for execution, they would pass through this Tower.

the transport of water for the imperial house. Early in the morning everyday, a caravan of carts loaded with water fetched from the fountain of the Yuquan Mountains would pass through this gate. No one was allowed to stop those carts. Of course there was other water for city folks. The trouble was that there were not many wells providing fine water. In certain areas, people had to manage with water that had a bitter taste.

Yuntai of the Juyong Pass (residence of the mediocre). It was said that when Emperor Qin Shi Huang was building the Great Wall he had a number of unskilled workers live here, hence the name. Yuntai was a place troops had to pass when entering Beijing from north.

Going north through the Yongding Gate at the southern end of the city, one would pass two imperial structures, Tiantan (Heavenly Altar) and Xiannongtan (Altar of Farming). Both were places for the emperor to offer annual sacrifices on special days. Going further north and passing

Chongwen Gate, also known as Hademen, was the office for the largest customs post in Beijing. Towards the end of the Qing dynasty, all the taxes collected here were barely enough to cover the expenditures on cosmetics for Empress Dowager, Ci Xi.

The Arrow Tower of Anding (Peace) Gate. It was here the emperors passed on their way back to Beijing from expeditions. They were fond of the auspicious name of this gate.

Xizhi Gate served as a special entry way for water carts bound for the Forbidden City. The water was spring water fetched from the Yuquan Hill (Jade Spring Hill) to be used only by the imperial house.

through Tianqiao, one would reach Zhushikou. There to the north stood the magnificent Arrow Tower. This tower was huge because it served as the southern entrance to the capital city when there was no outer city. Since it was a key stronghold for defense, it had to be solid and tall. To the north of this tower was the Qianmen Gate, which was also known as the Zhengyang Gate. These structures stood in between the inner city and the outer city. Their geographic location was extremely important. A large number of people came and went through this area.

To the north of the Zhengyang Gate there was a gate not very tall but most significant. During the Ming dynasty, it was called Daming Gate (Great Ming Gate). During the Qing dynasty, its name was changed to Daqing Gate (Great Qing Gate). The change of its name indicated its importance. After the establishment of the Re-

Zhengyang Gate after a snowfall.

public of China, it was changed to the Zhonghua Gate (Chinese Gate). It has, however, been pulled down and today no longer exists. It used to be the main entrance to the Imperial Palace. Behind this entrance was a T-shaped square known as Qianbulong (A Thousand Steps Corridor). It was through here that high-ranking officials passed on their way to court. Standing here and looking up, one could see the Tiananmen Tower in the north. To the north of the Tiananmen Tower is Ruimen Gate. Further north stands the Wumen Gate which is the central southern entrance to the Forbidden City.

The Arrow Tower of Qianmen Gate. Many of us got to know this structure from the picture printed on the cigarette package with the brand name "Great Qianmen".

The Daqing Gate (Great Qing Gate), also know as Zhonghua Gate (Chinese Gate), used to be the front gate to the Imperial Palace. Within this gate, there lay the T-shaped Qianbulong (A Thousand Steps Corridor) where generals and ministers waited to be summoned by the emperor.

The structure of the Wumen is most imposing. It has five towers with one being in the center. Therefore it is also known as the Five Phoenix Building. Despite its fine name, it was here in front of this structure that high-ranking officials were beheaded by the imperial

garrison at the order of an emperor. On such occasions, the fine-looking building was no longer so "imposing". Behind Wumen Gate stands Taihe Gate, and from south to north lie the Taihe Dian (Hall of Supreme Harmony), Zhonghe Dian (Hall of Central Harmony), and Baohe Dian (Hall of Preserving Harmony). These are at the center of the Forbidden City. It was in these halls that the emperor received ministers, held ceremonies, and handled state affairs.

Further to the north was the Qianqing Gate (Gate of Heavenly Purity), which served as the entrance to the inner palace. The northern part of the Forbidden City was where the Emperor and his families lived. Finally there is the Shengwu Gate at the northern end of the Forbidden City. Across a street lies the Jingshan Hill. On top of that hill towers a pavilion named the Wanchunting (Ten Thousand Springs Pavilion). From there one has a panoramic view of the whole city. To the north of the hill is the Di'an Gate, which used to be the northern gate to the Imperial Palace. Further north there is the Drum Tower and then, after a hundred meters, the Bell Tower, which is at the northern end of the axis of the city. There is no road to go further north. Instead, there are a series of densely distributed alleys running from east to west. In fact the density was needed for it was thought to block any "imperial air" from leaking out.

A bird's eye view of the capital. The axis of Beijing stopped at the Bell Tower in the northern end, which was believed to block the "imperial air" from leaking out.

leaking out.

Chapter 2
Capital of the Empire

"Gate" and "Way" to the altar of sacrifice.

The Eternal Axis

Guozijian (Imperial College).

The Beijing of today was originally built in one stretch during the early Ming dynasty. After Emperor Zhu Di (ruled from 1403 to 1424) assumed the throne in Nanjing, he felt that he lacked his own social foundation. Therefore he actively prepared to move the capital. After 13 years' preparation and construction, Beijing was by and large ready with the wall of its inner city, the Imperial Palace, streets, and residential areas. It was a city in the shape of a square (present-day inner city). He then issued a decree announcing the move to the new capital called Beijing.

Human beings pay a great deal of attention to south, east, north and west. The sun rises in the east and sets in the west thus completing a circle before it starts another day. It is cold in the north and warm in the south. And it takes only a short period of time to feel the change. The temperature of the southern hemisphere is just the opposite of that in the northern one, although living in China one is unable to feel this. As time goes by, east is deemed superior between the east and west; north is deemed superior between the north and south. Therefore, the Imperial Palace sits facing south.

No nation in the world lays so much emphasis on directions as China does. And within China, no city paid so much attention to directions as did Beijing of the past. First of all, it was the concept of conditions that created the capital culture. In return, the capital culture enriched the meaning of north, east, west and south. It was along an axis running from north to south that the construction of Beijing took place from the very beginning.

With the Great Wall at its back, the city of Beijing sits facing south, overlooking the whole of Central China. Similarly, emperors of the ancient days sat on their thrones facing south, overlooking all the provinces in the south. If we study ancient Beijing and

This city gate was named Daming Gate (Great Ming Gate) during the Ming dynasty and changed to Daqing Gate (Great Qing Gate) during the Qing dynasty. The government of the Republic of China then changed it to Zhonghua Gate (Chinese Gate). Today it no longer exists.

those emperors who lived in ancient Beijing, we are bound to find endless joy and quite interesting information.

The concept of north, east, west and south permeated into the life of commoners in ancient Beijing as well. They were very careful to be sure that what they did and what they said were in compliance with the norms of north, east, west and south.

For example, when a Beijinger selected a house whether for purchase or lease, he would first examine its quality and then in which direction it faced. For residence, a *siheyuan* would be the most ideal choice. But as a whole, the house should sit facing south. In those alleys running from east to west, half of the

The Son of Heaven followed the traditional rule of sitting on the throne facing south. Similarly, from small imperial path to the Golden Bridge in front of the Tiananmen rostrum, all structures were built facing south.

This is Yangxin Dian (Hall of Mental Cultivation), where Ci Xi once lived. Ci Xi (1835-1908), the imperial concubine of Emperor Xian Feng of the Qing dynasty, became the true ruler of the Qing Empire after 1861 when the emperor died.

Dongnuan Ge (Pavilion of Winter Warmth) of Yangxin Dian (Hall of Mental Cultivation). It was here Ci Xi held imperial sessions behind a curtain.

This is a yamen (a government office during feudal society), also facing south. It was here matters related with foreign countries were handled. It was the equivalent of the Ministry of Foreign Affairs of today.

Foxiang Ge (Tower of Buddhist Fragrance) of the Summer Palace.

houses face north whereas the other half face south. So there is a clear comparison between them. Normally, the price for those facing north would be lower.

Such a geographic concept has gradually produced some influential derivatives over the long years. For example, there is a saying that goes like this: "Those with money do not live in a house facing west," because only a house facing to the south is considered the best residence. A house facing north is always in shade. A house facing west has too much sunshine. And a house facing east would be next to a house facing south. Another saying is: "The yamen gate is open wide to the south; with right but no money, don't go inside." Yamen here means the office of a magistrate. All those yamens were backed by the emperor. Naturally, they all had to face south.

The imperial throne in Taihe Dian (Hall of Supreme Harmony). During the Qing dynasty, only great ceremonies such as the assuming of the throne, birthday celebrations, New Year celebrations, and the bestowing of important official titles were held in this hall.

A view of Kunming Lake as seen from Foxiang Ge (Tower of Buddhist Fragrance). This principal structure in the Summer Palace also faces south.

A photo of the Tiananmen rostrum taken in 1915.

Taihe Dian (Hall of Supreme Harmony) was the center of the Forbidden City. The throne carved with golden-colored dragons was the symbol of imperial power. The throne in this picture was used by Yuan Shikai when he became the self-styled emperor. When the imperial palace was turned into a museum in 1947, a dilapidated throne that had been used by several Qing emperors was found amidst a pile of old furniture in the warehouse of the Board of Internal Affairs to replace this one.

A Symmetrical Imperial City

Having discussed the axis, we can now talk about the symmetry between left and right. Chinese philosophy lays stress on balance and stability. Therefore, structures on the left and right of the axis should be by and large symmetrical. For example, along the axis from the Yongding Gate, through Tianqiao, Qianmen Gate, Tiananmen Gate, and Wumen Gate to the three halls in the north, the structures on both sides of these buildings are all balanced. The number of gates on the left and right are exactly the same. In the outer city, there is Tiantan (Heavenly Altar) in the east and Xiannongtan (Temple of Farming) in the west. In the inner city, there is Taimiao (Temple of Ancestors) in the east and the Shejitai (Altar of Land and Grain) in the west. Even in the throne hall of the Imperial Palace, civil officials stood on the eastern side and generals on the western side. It was likewise with a commoner's dwelling. If you entered such a dwelling, you would find that the dining room was situated on one side (the east), the toilet on the other side (the west). This was known as "kitchen on the left, toilet on the right". It was just as symmetrical as the city layout. The purpose of such a symmetrical arrangement was to accomplish balance and stability. However, this developed too. During the Yuan dynasty(1271-1368), the Left Prime Minister ranked higher than the Right Prime Minister. Again, in Peking operas performed in the Qing Court, important officials stood on the left whereas less important officials stood on the right. So left was superior than right. But it changed later. Today, it is right which is deemed superior than left.

Many of these ideas of Beijing folks in the old days have been discarded. The city planning of the old Beijing laid emphasis on vertical lines. One prominent example was the axis that ran from south to north. The symmetrical arrangement of structures also served the purpose of giving prominence to the axis. But today, horizontal roads have been built. First, there was Chang'an Boulevard. Then, a parallel road has recently been built, known as Ping'an

The pillar in Taihe Dian (Hall of Supreme Harmony) is so thick that it requires three people holding hands to encircle it. In order to fell such huge trees deep in the mountains, numerous people were forced to do the labor. A tree as large as this was extremely difficult to move after it was cut down. Added to the difficulties of obtaining such pillars was the fact that those mountains teemed with wild animals and snakes. The laborers suffered a great deal from hunger, illness, hard labor, etc. It was quite common for only five hundred out of a thousand people who did such work in the mountains to survive. The huge pillars eventually entwined with carved dragons resulted in countless widows.

Interior of Yikun Gong (Palace of the Queen Consort) in the Forbidden City.

Ave. Since China adopted the policy of opening to the outside world, the general city planning of Beijing has tended to fan out in all directions.

To cleave the ancient city in the middle so as to build a road was not an easy thing. Recently there was an article in a newspaper entitled "Ping'an Ave. cuts through cultural relics". It said that in each meter of earth to be dug up, there was a period of history. Several ancient tombs were excavated when the road was under construction. One day, when a bulldozer pushed down an old house, there appeared behind the house a most valuable screen wall originally erected by the government office headed by Duan Qirui. In the vicinities of Beihai, Xianliangci (Temple of Noble Men) and Baoanci (Peace-preserving Temple), the blueprint of the road had to be amended time and again because of such artifacts and the

Jiaotai Dian (Hall of Celestial and Terrestrial Union), in which the seals of the emperors of past dynasties were stored.

road building progressed gingerly.

Chang'an Boulevard used to be called "Heavenly Street". It was a 500-meter long thoroughfare running from east to west, constructed in front of the Chengtian Gate when Beijing was first built during the reign of Emperor Yong Le of the Ming dynasty. Both ends of this street had a city gate, named respectively Chang'an Left Gate and Chang'an Right Gate. Later on, Heavenly Street was renamed Chang'an Boulevard. This photo shows the archway to east Chang'an Boulevard that no longer exists today.

Tiananmen in 1912 when the provisional government of the Republic of China was founded.

A foreign-made mirror in Qianqing Gong (Palace of Celestial Purity) in the Forbidden City.

"Traces" Left by the "Sons of Heaven"

A piece of a gate. All those who have been to the Forbidden City find that carvings of dragons can be seen everywhere. Even the gates and windows are carved with dragons.

In Beijing, apart from its axis, there was a center. Geographically, this center was located at the northern end of the axis, close to the eastern side of Lake Jishuitan. Psychologically, in the feudal times, where the emperor appeared was always the center. So the center was changed from time to time. For example, when the emperor sat on the throne giving instructions at the morning session, the throne hall was the center of the imperial rule. In the afternoon, the emperor would go to his Southern Study where he would discuss important thorny issues with his close ministers. The Southern Study then became the center in which imperial decrees were prepared that would be announced the following day. In the evening, the emperor might go to bestow fortune on a certain imperial concubine. He would then be followed by his close secretary, a eunuch holding the "Record of Life". When the emperor entered the palace where the imperial concubine lived and closed the gate, the event would be recorded clearly in the "Record". Who could tell whether a future emperor might be produced that night.

Even though a center was selected when the city of Beijing was first built - on the eastern bank of Lake Jishuitan - in reality, the center kept moving backward or forward according to the whereabouts of the emperor. And the emperor spent most of his time in the rear palace. Before subservient eunuchs, he was the master. What he said went. Before his empress, consorts, imperial concubines, he was the only male. The place where he performed functions as the "Son of Heaven" was Taihe Dian (Hall of Supreme Harmony) in the front part of the Forbidden City. It was here that Heaven and the "human world" was divided. In front of his officials and generals in this hall, he made all decisions whether they were about policy-making or the appointment of officials. No matter what he said, it would be carried out without any conditions. If the

Caissons, pillars and the imperial throne in Taihe Dian (Hall of Supreme Harmony).

Empress Dowager Ci Xi in a sedan chair making an inspection of the Forbidden City.

emperor gave an order to put someone to death, even if that person was a minister on his knees in front of him, that person, on hearing the order, would have to thank the emperor. Even if the person was wrongly killed, no one would dare to protest. At most, at an appropriate later time, the victim might be retroactively given an official title and his families might be given some compensation in a roundabout way. That was it. There would be nothing more to be said.

Wherever one might be in Beijing, one would feel the existence of the axis, symmetry and the central point of the city. They had the function of cohesiveness and focus. In fact these served the purpose of highlighting the supremacy of the imperial power and the great importance of the emperor. The concept of the central point nourished and stimulated the concept of "I am the center". It was this belief that emperors adopted towards officials, and officials took towards the commoners. And among the commoners, the elderly adopted such attitude towards their children.

The stone ramp behind Baohe Dian (Hall of Preserved Harmony) weighs about 60 tons and is covered with carved dragons. It was transported to Beijing by several thousand people pulling and pushing it over ice made by pouring water along the way in winter. It is said that it took two months just to transport it a distance of a dozen kilometers.

Jingshan Hill is also known as "Coal Hill". On its top stands Wan Chun Ting (Ten Thousand Springs Pavilion), the highest building in the Forbidden City.

Overlooking Central China

A bird's eye view of the Forbidden City with its crowded buildings.

Persons visiting Beijing for the first time and suddenly finding themselves in Tiananmen Square would surely have the feeling that, "This is the capital. This is China," and he or she is its citizen. In the old days of the Ming, Qing and Republic of China periods, persons visiting Beijing for the first time and finding themselves in the center of the city would have a feeling that, "This is the imperial city" and he or she was its subordinate.

A capital must, first of all, be built in a good city, that should have a height from which one could have a panoramic view of that city. In the past such a place was Wanchunting (Ten Thousand Springs Pavilion) on top of the Jingshan Hill (also known as Coal Hill). Jingshang was the emperor's private garden and ordinary people were not allowed to enter. It was higher than the Imperial Palace, even higher than the imperial thrones in the three halls. Behind each throne, there was a screen. Ministers having a session with the em-

The throne in Qianqing Gong (Hall of Celestial Purity) where the emperor held sessions with his ministers and generals. The screen behind the throne was elaborately carved, highlighting the dignity of the emperor.

peror could see it. Common folks were, of course, not that fortunate. The screen served as a drop that highlighted the emperor's authority. The Jingshan Hill (Coal Hill) fanning out towards east and west also had the function of a screen for the imperial throne. Whenever people in the streets "looked up at random", they would see the Hill. Don't take this lightly. The moment they saw the Hill, they would feel the imperial power and an awe-inspiring emotion would rise in their hearts.

Wanchunting (Ten Thousand Springs Pavilion) on top of the Jingshan Hill was a geographic or physical vantage point. The political zenith was demonstrated here either by the handing down or changing hands of the imperial power. Every emperor had many sons. As a rule, the eldest son inherited the throne. This had been in practice for many dynasties. Generally speaking, no matter how senile an emperor might become, the Prime Minister would have to carefully abide by this rule. However, unexpected events did occasionally happen. An emperor might favor a younger son produced by a much-loved imperial concubine; or one of his younger sons, collaborating with some ministers, might usurp the throne. For instance, Emperor Yong Zheng of the Qing dynasty was the 4th son. How could he, of so many sons, assume the throne? The late emperor had written in his will that the 14th son was designated to assume the

This stone stele with words meaning "this is the place where Emperor Si Zong died for the State" indicates the location where the last emperor of the Ming dynasty hung himself. Emperor Si Zong, also known as Cong Zhen, ruled the country from 1628 to 1644.

throne. But the will was altered by the minister who was supposed to take care of the will. This is but a story, perhaps made up by someone who hated Yong Zheng. But what was strange was that two of his brothers who were most competitive died of unknown reasons. Therefore, the moment the old emperor was dying or when the new emperor was to assume the throne, there might be open strife and veiled struggle, or even murder. Normally, when an emperor died, the whole country, including Beijing, would have a long period of mourning. No recreational activities; no operas. No red color would be seen in the streets.

Sometimes, there were complex intrigues aimed at seizing power. One example was the struggle between Empress Dowager Ci Xi and Emperor Guang Xu. The

The throne in Qianqing Gong (Hall of Celestial Purity).

Qianqing Gong (Hall of Celestial Purity). When Li Zicheng led a peasant army and entered Beijing in 1644, Emperor Cong Zhen fled. There was a horizontal plaque with four characters meaning "be open and above board" hanging high on the wall of the hall. When an emperor was alive, he would write the name of his successor on a piece of silk and hide it in a box that would be placed behind this plaque. After the emperor died, a minister would break the seal on the box and announce the name of the new emperor.

These two photos show scenes at Yingtai in Zhongnanhai where Emperor Guang Xu was imprisoned by Empress Dowager Ci Xi.

former was a conservative while the latter was a reformist. Each had a large following. Ci Xi gained the upper hand and finally threw Guang Xu into a prison on a small island called Yingtai in Lake Nanhai. In order to cut all his contacts with the outside world, Ci Xi ordered the building of double walls around the prison. If it had been possible to go there to have a look, then we would better understand how miserable Guang Xu must have been. In the end, both of them came down with serious illnesses. However, each struggled to hold fast to life in the hope of outliving the other. The one lasting the longest would be able to seize the imperial power. It is said that the ailing Ci Xi asked eunuchs to carry her to Yingtai to see Guang Xu, who was then dying. Ci Xi and her nephew gazed at each other without a word. What was on their minds must have been extremely complicated. Guang Xu died first. That night, Ci Xi died too. Some people believe that Ci Xi sent someone to kill Guang Xu by poison when she realized that her own days were numbered. Recently people have been able to read the medical record of Guang Xu

This photo was taken in 1908, showing a funeral procession for deceased Ci Xi and Guang Xu.

written by an imperial doctor and have found the truth - Guang Xu had "died of his own illness".

After that, a number of important events took place in the leadership of China. In the year of 1911, the 1911 Revolution broke out in Wuchang; Sun Yat-sen (1866-1925) became the provisional president. The establishment of a Republic was the result of the natural development of society. Emperor Pu Yi (ruled from 1909 to 1911), the last emperor of China, resigned, ending once for all the feudal dynasties. Before long, Yuan Shikai (1859-1916) of Beijing, by resorting to treacherous means, virtually usurped all the power. Out of concern for the future of China, Dr. Sun decided to turn over the presidency to Yuan on condition that Yuan come

Ci Xi and her maids-in-waiting.

Foreign envoys and military attaches attended the funeral for Empress Dowager Ci Xi and Emperor Guang Xu.

to Nanjing to assume that post. When a group of representatives entrusted by Dr. Sun went to Beijing to invite Yuan to go south, Yuan manipulated his coup. He took this as an excuse, saying that he was unable to leave Beijing. Those representatives were hoodwinked and Dr. Sun's forces in Nanjing had no choice. Yuan Shikai thus became the Grand President in Beijing.

After that, there were endless struggles in Beijing over the restoration of the imperial system by Yuan Shikai. Cai E, Governor of Yunnan, ingeniously fled Beijing and returned home to Yunnan proclaiming his intention to overthrow Yuan. Yuan died in disgrace after being an emperor for just dozens of days. Zhang Xun, a loyalist to the Qing

Yuan Shikai, known as the "Usurper of the State".

dynasty, led his "Pigtail Troops" into Beijing in June, 1917, and announced the Restoration. For a couple of days, many Qing loyalists with pigtails sauntered along the Donghuamen Street. It was an eerie sight in the modern history of Beijing.

In 1924, Feng Yuxiang began a coup in Beijing that drove Pu Yi, who enjoyed special treatment in the Forbidden City, out of Beijing. Pu Yi had to run to Tianjin and there lived a reclusive life. Sun Yat-sen, despite his illness, went north to Beijing. There he made several public speeches that were highly acclaimed by the public. He passed away in Beijing. At first his coffin was buried in Biyun Si (Temple of Blue Clouds) in the western suburbs of the city. A few years later, it was moved to Nanjing. When the hearse moved from the

Sun Yat-sen, taken in Zhang Garden in Tianjin on his way to the north. It is said that this was his last portrait.

Yuan Shikai maintained the ritual of "offering sacrifices to Heaven" at Tiantan (Heavenly Altar).

Sun Yat-sen passed away in Beijing. This photo shows the funeral hall in Tieshizi Alley.

The funeral procession for Sun Yat-sen filed through Zhengyang Gate.

Temple of Blue Clouds and passed the Summer Palace to enter the city of Beijing, the streets were lined with tearful crowds of people, said to be an aggregate of several hundreds of thousands. This had never happened before in the history of Beijing.

If it were not for those "historical events", there would not be a Beijing today. The grandness and the unique atmosphere of an imperial capital would not be displayed either.

Taihe Dian (Hall of Supreme Harmony) in 1915. The flags hanging in the hall were those of the short-lived dynasty of Yuan Shikai.

A corner tower stood at the southwest corner of the Forbidden City behind Yat-sen Park, a park so named in memory of Sun Yat-sen. The park used to be known as the Central Park. Earlier than that it had been named Sheji Tan (Altar of Land and Grain).

Picture of a city gate of Beijing taken in the 1930s.

"Imperial Air" Must not Be Leaked out

    Not all Chinese cities have city walls and city gates. City walls and gates are not a criterion for an international city. Many famous cities abroad have never had such things. But almost all capitals in ancient China had city walls and gates. And in ancient times, capitals of many kingdoms had city walls and gates, though not as complete and elaborate as the later ones.

    The city walls and gates of Beijing, the last capital of feudal times in China, were the most complete and elaborate in China. The earliest walls were built with rammed earth covered with some straw mats on the outside in order to keep out rain or wind. It was after a long period that people developed the method for covering rammed earth with bricks. This method required quality bricks. Therefore it promoted development of the production of bricks and tiles. It was not easy to fire bricks for construction. The earth used to make brick bases had to be meticulously selected. Then it had to go through a complicated process. For instance, earth used for making bricks for the three halls in the Forbidden City had to be sifted through refining sieves. The fired bricks were then steeped in tong oil so that they could be polished smooth.

The form of the city wall and gates in ancient China probably had something to do with the typical Chinese idea of "using a neighbor's fields as a drain". When a person, a nation, or a state fared well, they would guard against encroachment from outside. At the same time, they would "wrap themselves up layer by layer". The poor common people lived in the outer city. Closer in were the middle class with some wealth and social status; then loyal bureaucrats; and the innermost part was for the emperor.

Such a distribution of residents was not done overnight. In the times of the Jin, the Imperial Palace was not located in the center of the city. It was not until the Yuan dynasty that the capital was established this way. Though the capital was moved and rebuilt during the Ming and Qing dynasties, the city planning was conducted in the same manner.

Wherever there was a city wall, there were gates for people to pass through. A gate needed some kind

A bastion of the Great Wall, which could be used to hide troops, store grains, shoot arrows and light alarm fires.

A street lined with shops.

of decoration, therefore, a tower was built. When there was a gate with a tower, it needed to be protected, hence the construction of a blockhouse. To make it impregnable, a moat was built outside the blockhouse. To guard against any enemy attacking at places where there were no gates nor moats, corner towers were erected at the four corners of the city on which troops could stand sentry duty.

Having said this, I think it is easy to understand why the city built structures like city gates, city walls, city towers, blockhouses, arrow towers, corner towers, etc. Those structures in Beijing are solid and magnificent, and are among the best examples of city structures in China as well as in the world.

The city of Beijing encircled with a wall and its gates was in the shape of a square. It overlooked the

A local street fair.

A corner tower and the moat.

South with an "imperial air". The city was particular about the number of its gates. During the Liao dynasty (916-1125), there were two gates on each of the four sides of the city. So there were eight gates. They were simple and well balanced. By the time of the Jin dynasty (1115-1234), the city had been enlarged and the gates were increased to thirteen: three gates on the east, west and south sides, and four gates on the northern side. In the case of the three gates on one side of a wall, one needed to be in the middle of that side. In the case of four gates, the side was divided into five parts and there was no gate in the middle. The capital, known as Dadu during the Yuan dynasty (1271-1368), was erected on a flat piece of land in a planned way, hence the birth of the most splendid city of that time in the world. It had eleven gates, three gates on each side of the east, west and south. The northern side had only two gates. What were the reasons for such an arrangement? Some elderly people thought that it would have been too chaotic to have four gates on the northern side. This was good because there was no middle gate. The emperor sat facing south and was able to look ahead of him indefinitely. He needed a solid wall at his back. At that time Beijing was well protected too. In the far north, there was the Great Wall. Right behind the Imperial Palace was Jingshan Hill. In between these was the northern wall without an entrance at its center. If there had been an opening in the middle of the wall, the "imperial air" would have leaked out.

During the Ming dynasty (1368-1644), the imperial capital was rebuilt. At first it had only an inner city. On both the eastern side and the western side, the three gates each were reduced to two. The total number of gates were thus reduced from thirteen to nine. The

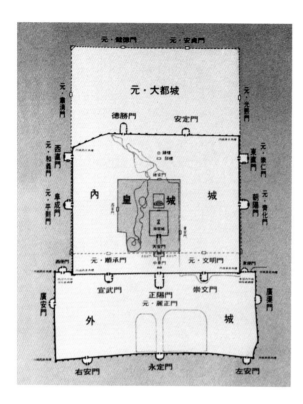

The city wall and gates of old Beijing were either renovated or enlarged during the Ming dynasty on the basis of the design for the capital known as Dadu of the Yuan dynasty. With the Forbidden City as its center, Beijing was composed of the area within the outer imperial walls, inner city and outer city. This map shows the locations of those walls and gates.

number "nine" was an auspicious figure in the eyes of the imperial house. Later on, there was a new title created: "Nine Gate Governor". An outer city was added later. The initial plan was that there would be a distance between the inner city and the outer city with another enclosure wall. When construction began, a financial problem propped up. The money for the wall had already been taken by the emperor to build temples. As a result, only half of the enclosure wall was roughly built in the south and it was connected with the wall of the inner city. However, the outer city was expanded from the inner city towards the south and had a symmetrical design. For this, another seven gates were added: three on the southern side, two on the northern side and one each on the western and eastern sides.

Part of the Great Wall was seriously damaged by the elements of nature and by human behavior so it no longer played its original function. It remained like a quiet reclining dragon along the undulating Yanshan Mountains.

Chapter 3
The Fall of the Dynasty

A photo of officers of the Eight Allied Forces taken in front of a palace gate.

Yuan Ming Yuan in Its Last Days

Tightly closed gate of the Forbidden City.

If you looked at the "Historical Beijing" from the sky, you would find that its structures were all built in a national style of architecture despite the class differences of the different areas. This remained unchanged for centuries. In the eyes of the owner of the Forbidden City, it was right and proper for him to be protected by several circles of walls and thus to enjoy supreme power. This was an unalterable principle since ancient times. Was there anything that needed changing? This was the supreme country, and all foreigners were outlandish and inferior. When they had some money in hand, they might want to enter this country to do business. No way! Some even indulged in such wild fantasies as to "borrow" some of China's ports. That was but daydreaming.

Yet who would have thought that opium would break open the door of the country. Even ministers became addicted. The emperor had no way but to proclaim a ban on opium. This led to the Opium War. What was least expected was that the Qing troops, which were said to be the most dauntless and fiercest army, met ignominious defeat shortly

A foreign warship demonstrated at Dagu Port in Tianjin in protest against the Qing Court.

On 17 June 1900, the Eight Allied Forces destroyed the cannon base at Dagu and then the troops headed for Tianjin.

after the breakout of the war. The weaponry of the foreigners was far superior. Foreign troops landed in Tianjin twice.

Tianjin, also known as "Jinmen Gate", provided an entrance to Beijing. How could it be tolerated to let foreign troops take Tianjin so easily? In reality, Dagu fell and then Tianjin was occupied. Gui Liang, a high-ranking official, signed traitorous treaties with Britain and France at the order of the emperor. The following year, the arrogant envoys of those two countries decided to go to Beijing to exchange the treaty texts. But they intended to enter Beijing by warship. An alarmed Emperor Xian Feng (ruled from 1851 to 1861) would not

The troops of the Eight Allied Forces were at the foot of the city wall of Beijing by August 1900.

Ruins of Chang Chun Yuan (Evergreen Garden), one of the three parts of Yuan Ming Yuan (Garden of Perfection and Brightness).

The Great Fountain and northern side of Jieqiqu (Hall of Strange Interest) in Changchun Yuan (Evergreen Garden) was destroyed by a fire.

allow this to happen. Immediately the British and French sent more troops. Dalian, Yantai, Dagu and Tianjin all fell into the hands of those foreign troops. Then they defeated the Qing troops at a place named Baliqiao in Tongzhou, outskirts of Beijing. Emperor Xian Feng fled the Forbidden City. The foreign troops raided and looted Yuan Ming Yuan (Garden of Perfection and Brightness). Whatever could be taken away from there was taken away by carts and animals. Whatever could not be removed was savagely destroyed. More than three thousand troops were then ordered to burn down the whole Yuan Ming Yuan. For several days and nights, its smoke enveloped the whole city. Thus the most beautiful garden in the world was burnt to ruins. Today, we can only imagine the extraordinary architectural masterpieces of this garden by looking at some old photos.

The platform of the second floor of the principal hall of Jieqiqu (Hall of Strange Interest).

The entrance to Dongjiao Minxiang, the legation area, was guarded by an Austrian soldier.

The French barracks at Dongjiao Minxiang.

Artillery on the wall of Dongjiao Minxiang, a legation area.

The Qing Emperor Learned A New Word: "Concession"

Empress Dowager Ci Xi, a wicked woman who ruled China for a long time, made China decline even further than it had before.

Ci Xi is a notorious figure in China. This is known even to children. When her nephew assumed the throne, she became the Empress Dowager. She worked hand in glove with Prince Gong, Yi Xin to plan a coup. She killed the eight ministers who had been entrusted by the deceased emperor to look after the young emperor. After that she held court from behind a screen for scores of years and signed a number of traitorous treaties with foreign countries. She was fearful of the Reformists and therefore put a number of renowned Reformists to death. Finally she threw Emperor Guan Xu, who backed the Reform, into jail. She tried to maintain her rule at the expense of deterioration of the country. She hated any request made by the foreigners to return the power to the emperor. She made use of the Boxing Movement, which rose to struggle against foreign imperialism, to fight against the foreigners. She hoped this would weaken both the Boxers and the foreigners so that she might gain the benefits. But steel knives

Portrait of Emperor Guang Xu.

Portrait of Kang Youwei, who turned from being a leading reformist into a royalist.

Portrait of Tan Citong, a leading radical reformist.

A foreign bank in the concession.

were no match for foreign guns and cannons. Soon Tianjin fell and the Eight Allied Forces attacked and entered Beijing. Ci Xi fled to Xi'an, leaving the Forbidden City to the foreigners. This has left us a great many worn-out photos showing those foreign robbers reviewing troops in formation, or jauntily doing exercises in the Forbidden City. This has certainly broadened our vista and, at the same time, made us indignant as well as shamed.

In order to show her "repentance" for "offending" the foreigners, she ordered that the Boxing Movement be wiped out. In her eyes, the foreigners knew little about rites. Before the completion of negotiations, they occupied Dongjiao Minxiang Street near the Forbidden City, built Western-style buildings, barracks and embassies. Foreign flags fluttered in front of those structures; sentries were posted at their gates. Chinese were barred from

A bird's-eye view of Dongjiao Minxiang.

Some of the Qing troops who fought against foreign religions and foreign invaders together with the Righteous Harmony Corp (Yi He Tuan, or Boxers).

entering the street. Only then did Ci Xi and her ministers learn the new word "concession".

In the concession, there was not an inch of land belonging to China; the Qing government had no power there. It was a foreign country within a country. Ci Xi and her followers had to accept the situation. She, however, became cleverer as a result. She once made a

A member of the Righteous Harmony Corp (Yi He Tuan, or Boxers) being arrested.

A scene of Dongjiao Minxiang destroyed by the Boxers, taken in 1900.

Photo of solders of the Eight Allied Forces with Chinese prostitutes, published in a newspaper of the time with this caption: Close relations between China and the West.

Photo of Japanese soldiers taken in front of the burned-down mansion of Prince Su after the fall of Beijing.

statement that later became well known: "With the resources of China, we will be able to please all states." To put it in plain words, she decided to trade off part of the sovereignty for her rule of the country. To the rulers of the Qing dynasty, it was worth it. Another famous saying of hers was: "Give it to foreign states rather than home slaves." What she meant was that an uprising of the common people would be more dangerous than foreign aggression.

Portrait of Sai Jinhua, a controversial woman of Chinese modern history.

Headquarters and barracks of the Japanese troops of the Eight Allied Forces that occupied Beijing.

Embassies and barracks at Dongjiao Minxiang of the invading armies of Britain, Japan, and Holland.

Chapter 4
Streets and Alleys

A stone bridge linking Lake Beihai and Lake Zhonghai, and an archway at one end of the bridge.

Old Archways in Photos

Archways in various architectural designs were attractive scenes in old Beijing.

The layout of the old Beijing did not remain unchanged over the years. For example, during Liao times (916-1125), the city was divided into 26 *fangs* (districts). Each *fang* had an archway on which were written the name of the *fang* such as Lulong, Yongping, Tangyin, etc. This was an outcome of the district market system of the Tang dynasty (618-907). Within each *fang*, the residents engaged by and large in the same trade, and the work they did was highly specialized. In each *fang*, there were several *shanlans* (fences). According to the historical record, there were a total of 1090 *shanlans* in Beijing. The existing Dashanlan near Qianmen Gate of today was one of those *shanlans*. During the daytime, the railing gate was open and the street was available to the public. During the night, the railing gate was closed and curfew was declared. The function of each *fang* was quite different, and residents in a *fang* had to live by bartering their trades. All was quite primitive.

By the late Qing and early Republic periods, the

"district market" system had come to an end. All the *fangs* were changed to "districts". At the beginning, there were five districts, namely, the East District, West District, South District, North District and Central District. Later, these were merged into the East City District and West City District in the inner city and the Xuanwu District and the Congwen District in the outer city. The control of each *fang* over the freedom of its residents disappeared. They were no longer limited to living within the *fang* in which their forefathers had lived for generations and a son did not have to follow his father's step in choosing a career. People were free to choose their residences as well as careers. Markets of all kinds mushroomed; temple fairs, apart from their commercial functions, became places for rest and recreation. Obviously the city had made progress.

Archways could be found in streets and gardens of old Beijing. They were made of wood, stone, carved bricks or glazed bricks. Many of them collapsed or were removed to give way to city development. Not many still exist. The photo shows the Dongdan Archway as it appeared in 1916.

Of course, districts in Beijing did not remain unchanged. After completion of the building of the outer city, Qianmen became not only the geological center of the city but also the most prosperous business center. But how to administer Qianmen? This was a headache to the rulers. Qianmen District had been founded three times in the mid-Qing dynasty, the period of the Republic and the early days of the People's Republic of China, respectively. Later on, it was divided into two and merged into Xuanwu District and

Chongwen District.

Today, not many features of the old Beijing have remained unchanged, and very often they seem out of place in the new era. However, the landscape of old Beijing has given us so many memories. They are thought provoking and make us think what is wrong and what is right.

The archway on Qianmen Street taken in March 1940.

This is a drawing executed by a foreign artist. The building structures and patterns on the wall, people's clothes and other objects are meticulously painted. However, the people's faces are like those of Westerners.

Hutongs

Dongsi Archway.

Wherever one stood, he would find that residential areas were cut crisscross by streets. The residences along those streets were the basic units. And the residences could be divided into various classes. There were strict rules in regard to them. The largest and the most magnificent one was the Imperial Palace. Next came mansions for princes and then the luxurious dwellings in which lived either officials or big merchants. These were followed by *siheyuan* (a compound with houses around a courtyard), which again could be divided into many different classes. After that came the little courtyards that were not necessarily enclosed by buildings on four sides. Finally there were the courtyards with disarrayed houses, known as *dazayuan*, which could be found everywhere in the city.

Buildings were constructed in groups. If one looked at the city from some high point, one would find differences in their roofs. Yellow tiles were reserved for the roof of the Imperial Palace, green tiles for prince

The contrast of a small, poor community and the mansion of a prince.

mansions. The roofs of all gate towers were laid with gray cylindrical tiles and edged with green tiles. In the case of ordinary residences, the roofs were all laid with gray tiles. In Beijing, one could never breach the rules relating to the color of the walls and roofs, the height of a house, the thickness of rafters, the size of the entrance gate, the shape and pattern of the horse-mounting stones, etc., or one would be committing a crime that merited the death penalty.

Different groups of housing were separated by streets and alleys. The widest of these in Beijing were called streets while the narrow ones were called hutongs. Hutong is a unique name for small streets in Beijing. They are narrower than streets, and run both horizontally and vertically. Similar narrow streets also exist in Shanghai and other cities. There they are called longtangs. The two of them are different as far as their characteristics are concerned. Longtangs could form a network fanning out in a zigzag pattern, not subject to direction, length or straightness. Hutongs were something else. They were a basic component of the city. Streets in Beijing run straight either from west to east

The study of Prince Li, the second son of Nurhaci. The garden was built later. But it has long since been demolished.

or south to north. They are very neat. Similarly, the hutong had the same characteristics. A hutong normally runs parallel to a nearby street. Its length is just the same as the street.

Most Beijingers were born in a hutong, and grew up in a hutong. So if a Beijinger strolled on such a narrow, stifling hutong, he would undoubtedly have a whole map of Beijing in his mind.

Children grew up in the hutong.

Since all streets ran either from west to east or from south to north, each turn on a street would be in the shape of a right angle. No matter what route one might take, the total length to reach a destination was the same. However, different routes had different scenery. Some people might like a quiet surrounding, others might be fond of busy streets. Their choices of routes to get to the same place might differ. However, Beijing today does have a few diagonal streets such as Widow Ma Slant Street. If you happen to have a diagonal street leading to your destination, you will have a short cut.

Nearby alleys were connected to one another, thus forming a little community. Even if you stayed away from busy streets for a couple of months, your life would not be affected. Little shops in those alleys would have everything you might need. Besides, people living in the same community knew one another well.

A scene in a hutong.

You would probably feel comfortable doing a little transaction with someone you knew. If you happened not to have any cash with you, the shop owner would say, "Take them home first. When you have time, just drop in and pay for them."

How did people dispose of unwanted things? Rubbish collectors would come and buy old, worn-out clothes and unwanted objects. With a little parcel under his arm, a rubbish collector would tattoo on a little drum as large as his palm with a long tassel on it, while shouting as he walked, "Any rubbish - I'll pay for it!" As for sewage, cleaners carrying cylindrical containers on their backs visited each household and removed it.

When a battle took place in a city, both sides would first control strategic points and major streets. But hutongs would often be neglected. Deep in those hutongs, there were seedy things of course. However they often produced "dragons" and "tigers". When a man was chased by some robbers, his neighbor would readily let him cross over the wall and hide him in his house. This indicates that Beijingers had a sense of justice.

Owner of a tobacco shop.

From the end of the Qing dynasty to 1935 the main currency that circulated was copper coins. There was no fixed exchange rate between silver and copper coins, so one silver coin could be changed for 100 copper coins in the early days of the Republic, and for 300 copper coins later. Therefore, money exchangers like this one in the photo proliferated so as to glean profits through such exchanges.

Ladies of a rich family enjoyed themselves by playing cards.

Rickshaw boys waiting for customers.

Hutongs could be quite different in appearance. Some were wide and neat, their residents shuttled by carriages. Some were deserted and had dirty, pock-riddled road surface. Hutongs in the northern part of the city were better built than those in the southern part. But strangely, no matter where one lived in a hutong, they would not move out of it. Because once you got along well with your neighbors, you would have a feeling of safety and comfort. That would be more important than earning more money. So it was not rare for a family to live in the same place for generations. Craftsmen in particular (and also performers of Peking opera) mostly inhabited the hutong alleys near Caishikou in the

Xuanwu District. Since these were small, the residents saw renowned figures of their trade come and go. If one wanted to learn some "real art", they could just knock at the door of their neighbors. When the coaching was over, they might be invited to have a bowl of noodles with bean paste and meat shreds.

A person who lived in a hutong for a long period and became very familiar with the place and felt at home there was called Hutong *chuanzi*. Similarly, people called those who were engrossed in local operas *xichongzi* or *xiluozi*. If one stayed in the same old place, one might never be able to improve his situation. If he had the courage to leave the hutong, he would miss it when he had a moment of repose, no matter how far away he was from home.

A carved stone drum was usually placed at the gate of a rich family.

Different kinds of gates indicated the different social status of the home owners. The lintels of those gates accordingly were also different.

Street full of streamers bearing the names of the stores.

Step by Step, Just No Hurry

Foreign-style building standing in the downtown area - New World Tower.

It was not very accurate, I am afraid, to use the term "district" to divide Beijing as far as people's characteristics were concerned. The word "area" mentioned before perhaps would be most precise.

By "area", I mean a section of the city with a prominent feature. Take business areas for example. There were three renowned business areas. Qianmen Avenue, which included Dashanlan, was the most prosperous traditional business area. Dashanlan Street was the busiest street lined with all kinds of stores. The top stores of all trades would do their best to secure a place here. Besides, there were a few streets selling particular commodities in this area: jade ware in Langfang Ertiao Street, hats and shoes in Xianyukou, embroidery in Xihuying. In the old days, different shops hung different horizontal signboards and streamers written with words indicating the commodities they provided. Each had its own business. No one could pull the rug out from under another's feet or guilds would come to interfere.

The second leading business area was Wangfujing. The rise of Wangfujing came slightly later than Qianmen. However, it began at a higher level. Its Dong'an Market was one of its unique features. This was a disorderly bazaar selling all sorts of things. It was full of small restaurants, stalls and shops selling daily necessities, snacks, books, and odds and ends. In spite of the disorderly layout, the bazaar did have its own order. However, an outsider would never be able to make head nor tail out of it. Each time a customer visited the market, he would enjoy browsing among the commodities in such a place. Take secondhand books for example. One might have come here to look at books at random and would suddenly be delighted by finding something he had been long looking for. This is really a case of "to wear out a pair of iron shoes looking for it without success, but it suddenly appears with no effort."

The third business area was Tianqiao, a paradise for the poor.

Apart from the above three business areas, Beijing had a few places for temporary social gatherings - temple fairs.

I will come to that later. Lake Shishahai in the West District was a rare expanse of water for ordinary

Damuochang, a business center in old Beijing.

Workshops that produced lanterns especially for the imperial palace, government offices and shops.

In the downtown area of old Beijing there were various shops selling secondhand clothes, books, antiques, and groceries, as well as noodle restaurants and wine shops. There were all sorts of things available for sale in this street, which looked quite chaotic in appearance.

people…. Each area was a world of its own. Qianmen was a world, Wangfujing was another. Tianqiao was a third world. If we look at them in another angle, the circle of officials was a world. The circle of banking and finance was another. Even beggars formed their own well-knit world, which was incomprehensible to ordinary people.

In the areas of the Three Gates, namely, Xuanwu Gate, Qianmen Gate and Chongwen Gate, there used to

Beijing street in the 1930s.

Heng Tong Tea Shop, a renowned place of business for a century.

be many biaoju that provided escorts and bodyguards, which were to be found in some guilds. They served as escorts for the transport of valuable goods of the rich. There were hard *biaoju* and soft *biaoju*, the guards of the former living on their reputations for skill in marshal arts, and the latter being responsible to buy off feasible robbers along the route of transport. In the area from Caishikou to Hufangqiao of the Xuanwu District lived many opera actors and actresses, as well as mediocre and low prostitutes.

People resided in the various areas of Beijing from generation to generation. They became quite familiar with the area they lived in; and the areas nurtured their residents. Many such areas had their own characteristics. Let's consider the mental outlook of the Beijingers who "walked" in those areas.

First, as I mentioned above, Beijingers were very

Post offices began to appear in the 1920s. This one, which opened in the Board of Civil Service Street in 1922, looked quite impressive. Here are the photos of its façade and the interior. The old-fashioned vehicle was the first motor vehicle to transport the post.

A place by the water in old Beijing.

conscious of directions. When asked about a place, a Beijinger would say, "Go south and pass two blocks, then turn east and cross three Hutongs, you can't miss it." You would never hear this manner of talking in other cities of China.

Second, each Hutong contained a large number of Hutong *chuanzi*. What is Hutong *chuanzi*? It is mostly a negative term, referring to some of the youngsters who lived in the Hutong, idling away their time day in and day out. These youngsters did not work, yet were able to exist on the charity of their families. Some even had well-off lives. They got so used to living in the Hutong that when they looked at streets, prince mansions, or even the Imperial

The mule-pulled cart was a common means of transport in old Beijing.

Fashionable women in the late 1920s.

Palace, they would act as if these were Hutongs too.

Third, since Beijing had only a few diagonal streets, a pedestrian normally had to make right angles when he had to turn from one street to another. There was no shortcut. Therefore, Beijingers were usually straightforward by nature and never did anything in a "diagonal" (tricky) manner. When a Beijinger encountered anything unjust, he would definitely interfere, even if at the cost of his life. "When the surface of a road is not even, just scrape it flat!"

Fourth, Beijing had numerous streets and alleys. There were numerous people standing idly along the sides of such streets and alleys. Not many people walked in haste with their eyes focused straight ahead. The pace of life for Beijingers was relatively slow. Everything followed its old rut. Even very thorny matters would be dealt with step by step, not to say things of someone else's concern.

Sai Jinhua, a famous prostitute, in 1902.

To protect their own interests, many guilds were founded by craftsmen and handicraftsmen. Members of those guilds formulated their own rules.

A small street by a river outside Yongding Gate.

Chapter 5
Morning Bell and Evening Drum

A bird's-eye view of the Drum Tower and Bell Tower.

Wordless Sound

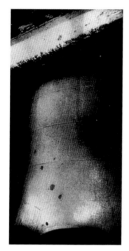

The huge bell in Juesheng Si (Temple of Awakening), also known as Great Bell Temple.

"Morning bell and evening drum" cannot be simply interpreted as "sound the bell in the morning" and "beat the drum in the evening". Instead, this is a kind of culture. Beijing has a Bell Tower and a Drum Tower. In the old days, the bell and the drum would be beaten when day broke and when dusk fell to tell people the time.

If you stood in Wanchunting (Ten Thousand Springs Pavilion) on top of the Jingshan Hill and looked in the direction of north, the first thing you might see would be the Drum Tower. It stood at the northern end of the city axis. It was first built in 1420 and then rebuilt twice in 1800 and 1894 respectively. The structure, erected on a high brick-laid platform, had two sloping roofs with a ridge in the center. The roofs were covered with gray cylindrical tiles with edges of green glazed tiles. There used to be twenty-five drums (one large drum and twenty-four small ones) on the second floor. At the first watch every evening, they would be beaten 108 times in two rounds. They would then be beaten 108 times at each watch until the fifth watch (five o'clock in the morning) which was known as the "daybreak watch". The drum beating had to be rhythmic. "Eighteen in quick tempo, eighteen in slow tempo and another eighteen not too quick and not too slow." That was the way drummers did it.

A hundred meters to the north of the Drum Tower towered the Bell Tower that sat at the northern end of the central axis of the city. It was first built in 1420 and an iron bell was placed here. Since this was not resonant, the iron bell was later replaced by a bronze bell weighing 42 tons. At seven o'clock every evening, the bell sounded for the first watch. It sounded again at five o'clock the following morning as the "daybreak watch". Each time it was rung 108 times. Residents, officials, and troops in the capital went to bed at the sound of the evening bell and rose at the sound of the morning bell.

The axis of Beijing extended through this arch of the Drum Tower.

It was ten hours' sleep from seven o'clock in the evening to the five next morning. People today might wonder if it was too long. Of course, not each household would be able to sleep for ten hours. But the ancient life style of "rising as the sun rises and resting as the sun sets" was still very influential among the residents of the capital. Night was a sensitive period to people and, therefore, it was separated by watches intoned by the sound of the drum and bell.

Zhu Jiajin, a man in his eighties, recently said when recalling his childhood, "I remember I could hear the sound of the drum and the bell every evening. The tempo was slow at the beginning and then turned fast, and repeated like this for three times. It was said to be 108 times, but I never counted. The drum was followed by the bell. The drum was beaten at midnight and again at the dawn. The sound was agreeable yet awe-inspiring. I often heard such words, 'Stop messing about now. It's time to go to bed. Don't you hear the drum?' I rarely heard the midnight drum. When

The Bell Tower was first built during the reign of Emperor Yong Le of the Ming dynasty. It was destroyed later by a fire and then rebuilt as a brick structure during the Qing dynasty. The bell announced the time for Beijing residents.

I heard it I was rather scared. I don't know why."

It was a wordless sound, an enlightening lesson for children. Why was the midnight drum scary? It was because all was so quiet at night. The sound of the drum seemed to have come from Heaven, representing the will of God. It ruled the common folks and also the emperor, as if telling him that there would be a morning session with officials next day and there should be a limit to indulgence... To ordinary people, when the drum sounded at the first watch, adults would urge their children to go to bed. So the sound of the drum left indelible impression on children's minds. When they grew older, they might have to burn the midnight oil for studies. So when the midnight drum sounded, they might go into the courtyard to practice swords in the moonlight so as to get refreshed.

The Drum Tower and the Bell Tower long ago stopped performing such functions. Today Dazhong Si (Big Bell Temple) is the only place that houses a large bell that sounds on the eve of the Chinese New Year. This temple is located in the Third Ring Road North. People in the vicinity can hear it when it is sounded, but the sound does not go very far.

Beijing is today very large, so large that the drum and the bell are unable to play the role they once played. Most cities in China have no drum tower or bell tower. So what do people miss most after a period of life in old Beijing? I bet it must be the sound of the drum and the bell.

Among the six ancient capitals, not all of them had a drum tower or the bell tower. Only Beijing, Xi'an and Nanjing had a drum tower and bell tower. If this is regarded as a criteria, these cities should be regarded as the first class capitals. The rest were the second class

Jia Liang in front of Taihe Dian (Hall of Supreme Harmony) was a standard measurement instrument of ancient China.

capitals. If you ask me about the value of the drum tower and the bell tower, I would say that they were objects with feelings. It set the rules for the ancient people providing a "regular life" and a "pattern for doing things".

You might ask, "Wasn't it boring and monotonous to hear the drum and the bell day after day? Would the residents become fed up living and working in such an environment?"

Yes, that might be true for people of today because they have accepted and are used to a busy metropolitan life. As for the people living in Beijing seventy or eighty years ago, and "at the foot of the Emperor", they would not. Though there was only one place that had the morning bell and the evening drum, there were drums and bells of a lower class in some monasteries and Taoist temples in Beijing. At funerals for instance, monks or Taoist priests would be invited to the home of the deceased to perform certain rituals by beating some musical instruments and reciting sutras. Such cer-

This sun dial was a device to mark time.

The bell in the Bell Tower sounded in the evening everyday. It sounded again at daybreak the following morning, hence the saying, "go to bed on hearing the bell, get up on hearing the bell."

In the Bell Tower time was calculated and marked by a bronze sand-glass made during the Song dynasty. This was lost in the Yuan dynasty. During the Ming and Qing times, incense was used to mark time. Although this was a poor method for getting the correct time, it remained unchanged for several dynasties.

emonies were also fun to watch. When such a ritual was carried out, drums and bells together would make resonant sounds. Of course there were other musical instruments too. In some recreational grounds, one might occasionally see someone playing more than ten musical instruments all by himself, including drums and bells with his hands and feet. Apparently, the person would be "selling" something. This was no longer art but a kind of acrobatics.

Beijingers had quite a number of places to go to enjoy themselves. During the day, there were temple fairs. In the evening, there were theaters staging local operas. Such entertainment was exciting. However, when the time came, the Drum and the Bell would remind them, "Haven't you heard the sound,

The Bell Tower in Nanjing during the Ming dynasty stood on top of a hill. It did not lie on the axis of the city.

The Bell Tower of Xi'an stood in the center of the city.

everyone? It's time you went home. Let's have a break for today. There'll be work for you tomorrow."

Bells were often seen in temples or government offices.
They were used on occasions for ritual ceremonies.

An elaborately built mosque near Anding Gate. This photo was taken in 1939.

Religion, a Walking-stick for the Ruler

Pagodas in Zhenjue Si (True Awakening Temple).

In feudal society, religion served as a walking-stick for the ruler. If the ruler walked unsteadily, the "body of the power" might slip. So a walking stick was quite handy to keep him from falling. When a man was in despair, particularly when he was on the verge of mental breakdown, he might find solace in religion. His pains would be temporarily gone or at least alleviated. Such an effect was of course sought after by both the rulers and the ruled of a feudal society. This provided a basis for the spread of religion in Beijing.

Why then did religion hold people spellbound? Scriptures? Moral ethics and the reputation of a religious leader? Magnificence of religious structures? A long history of a religion? These are all correct. However, there was also a record of miracles that surrounded a few temples of Beijing. For instance, in the courtyard of Tanzhe Si (Pool and *Zhe* Tree Temple) in the suburbs of Beijing, there towers a 27-meter-high ginkgo tree of a thousand years of age. It is said when a new

Beijing was a city full of temples, and religions flourished there. One reason for this was that the emperors all tried to strengthen their rule by making use of the various religions.

Tanzhe Si (Pool and *Zhe* Tree Temple) was so named because of the *zhe* trees in front and the stream at the back. It existed as early as the West Jin dynasty, 1,800 years ago. No wonder people said, "Tanzhe Si came first, Youzhou Town appeared later." Youzhou Town was the predecessor of Beijing.

emperor assumed his throne, an offshoot would sprout out beside this huge tree. It would grow to a height of three meters within a year. When an emperor died, the trunk of its offshoot would break open and gradually merge with the main trunk of the tall tree.

All in all, in places where religious practices were popular there were inevitably many sorts of tales. Since some phenomena beyond comprehension at the time, religion would provide people with certain explanations whether they were believed or not. And most people would believe them.

Jingang Baozuo Ta (Diamond Throne Pagoda) was added to the Biyun Si (Temple of Azure Clouds) in 1748, the 13th year of the reign of Emperor Qian Long. Both the base and the pagoda itself were built with white marble. The whole structure was carved in relief with images of Buddha, heavenly warriors, dragons, phoenixes, lions, elephants and clouds.

Coexistence of Buddhism, Taoism and Confucianism

Jade statue of Buddha.

In old Beijing, the influence of Buddhism was, of course, the greatest. It taught people to "do good deeds for the sake of the next life". There were a number of temples in Beijing. Fayuan Si (Temple of the Source of the Law) was built in the 19th year of the reign of Emperor Zhen Guan of the Tang dynasty (AD 645). It had formerly been called Minzhong Si (Temple of Compassion for Loyalists) and was renovated during the Ming dynasty (1368-1644). Another temple known as Guangji Si (Temple of Vast Succor) was built during the Jin dynasty (1115-1234). The structures in this temple are exquisite and beautiful. Its courtyards are quiet and secluded. There are also Guanghua Si (Temple of Broad Charity), Fahua Si (Temple of Power of Law), Xizhao Si (Sunset Temple), Tianning Si (Temple of Heavenly Peace, Dajue Si (Great Awakening Temple), etc. The rich people set up elegant, tranquil shrines at home and it was convenient for them to burn joss-sticks and recite scripture there. In many secluded alleys, there

Joyful Buddha (*huan xi fo*), also known as the duel-body (mating) statue of Buddha, housed in Yonghe Gong (Harmony and Peace Palace Lamasery).

Falun Dian (Law Wheel Hall) of Yonghe Gong (Harmony and Peace Palace Lamasery).

Serene and Pure Pagoda in Xihuang Si (West Yellow Temple).

stood some simple little temples. Beijingers would "make do" even in the case of religious beliefs.

The largest Taoist structure in Beijing is Baiyunguan (Temple of White Clouds). It was first built during the reign of Emperor Kai Yuan (714-741) of the Tang dynasty (618-907). It was here that Lao Zi was worshipped. Taoism advocates "tranquility and inaction". It was quite attractive to those who were fed up with the world of vanity. Not like Buddhism, it did not request physical self-restrictions on its followers. Therefore it had a big following. In Beijing there is another temple called Dongyue which was also frequented by many visitors. It was also a place for occasional temple fairs.

A young Taoist.

A family that was well-off would likely build a shrine at home to practice Buddhism. This photo shows one in the imperial palace.

Yonghe Gong (Harmony and Peace Palace Lamasery) is a base for Lamaism, a branch of Buddhism. With a large number of followers in Tibet and Inner Mongolia, it is rather prominent in Beijing. The location of this lamasery used to be the mansion of Yong Zheng (ruled from 1723 to 1735) before he took the throne. When he died, his coffin was laid in this place too. Every year, a festival known as "Striking Ghosts" is held here. This provides an opportunity for fun for the local folks. The proper name of this festival is "*tiaobuzha*", which, in Mongolian, means "driving away ghosts". In the east wing of Yonghe Gong, there is a statue of a couple mating, which is called *huan xi fo* (Joyful Buddha), reflecting the Buddha's human nature. It is said there are altogether five such statues housed in the monastery.

Donghuang Si (East Yellow Temple) and Xihuang Si (West Yellow Temple) are located outside Anding Gate. Those two temples are connected yet different in layout. Envoys sent by the Dalai and Panchan Lamas would usually stay here when they came to Beijing. The sixth Panchan died of smallpox in Beijing when he came to celebrate the

Yonghe Gong (Harmony and Peace Palace Lamasery) was the center of Lamaism in Beijing. In February every year, a ceremony was held here to expel evil spirits and monsters. According to the belief, heavenly warriors would catch and kill them at the order of Sakyamuni.

birthday anniversary of Emperor Qian Long (ruled from 1736 to 1795). To commemorate the sixth Panchan, Qian Long built a Clothes and Hat Tower in his honor.

The white dagoba in Baita Si (White Dagoba Temple) located in Fuchengmennei is said to have been designed by a Nepalese. It was built in the Yuan dynasty (1206-1368) and was named Miaoying Si (Temple of Resourceful Response) during the Ming dynasty (1368-1644). This is the largest Lama dagoba in China, particularly valuable for its architecture.

The Cattle Street Mosque (Niujie Libai Si) is the largest mosque with the longest history in Beijing. According to historical records, it was built during the Liao dynasty (907-1125). In architecture, it is based on ancient Chinese buildings, and contains Islamic decorative art. To scholars, Confucianism was on a par with a religion. In order to climb up in the hierarchy, scholars had to be pious and study Confucianism as though it was a religious belief. Guided by Confucianism, they worked hard in order to win an official title. In Beijing, there is a Confucius temple, a place worshipped by scholars. Next to this temple is Guozijian (Imperial College), also a place respected greatly by scholars in the old days.

Lamas reciting sutras in Yonghe Gong (Harmony and Peace Palace Lamasery). Such garments were unique to Tibetan Buddhists.

A little shrine hidden amidst the thick foliage on the outskirts of Beijing. On the plinth stood a Hindu god.

Women of Gentle Character and Men with a Sense of Justice

In the eyes of Buddhists, Avalokitesvara is a Goddess of Mercy. But those who long to have children regard her as the "Goddess of Sending Children".

More closely related to ordinary people than Confucian scholarship or religious theology were the characters of Guan Yin (Bodhisattva) and Lord Guan, both of whom were semi-human and semi-immortal. In an enclosure outside the Qianmen Gate, there used to be two small but significant temples, one housing a statue of Guan Yin, the other housing Lord Guan. Why did they build two temples in a business center of Beijing? Guan Yin had originally been a male god. But to ordinary people, Guan Yin was more a lady of grace. Sometimes Guan Yin was regarded as "Goddess of Children", which was indeed out of a practical purpose. Lord Guan is one of the heroes in the classic novel *The Romance of Three Kingdoms*. Many legends about Lord Guan made him a symbol of justice and righteousness. On the one hand, Lord Guan was an immortal. On the other, he was a model of behavior for ordinary people. In the old days, any one performing the role of Lord

Guan on the stage must be pious to the Lord or he would be punished by the spirit of Lord Guan. There is an interesting story about the renowned actor Yang Xiaolou who excelled in performing the role of a young man with martial arts. He rarely played the role of Lord Guan. Once he was invited to play this role, he decided to try once. After the performance, he had a headache. He blamed himself, believing that he was not pious enough and therefore being punished. Later on, he found out that it was the hat string which had been too tight on his head.

As time passed, Westerners turned their eyes to the East. Catholics entered China and acquired the right to do missionary work. Several Catholic churches were built in Beijing. Beijingers called them respectively "Southern Church", "Northern Church", "Eastern Church" and "Western Church" according to their locations.

Statue of Guan Yu. Guan Yu enjoys high esteem and stories about him are known to everyone in China because of the successful description of him in the famous classic novel *The Romance of Three Kingdoms*. He has become a symbol of loyalty and justice.

All this shows that there was no impassable chasm between religion, art and life. Zen, in particular, was most enlightening to the development of literary creation. Those who were quick to learn and used their brains would be able to "steal" things from religions. Those who did not use their brains and treated religions as if they were reading

A scene of Dongyue Temple.

This statue of an Arhat, not like others that are usually very serious, looks humorous and amusing.

books without understanding would not be able to succeed in either religion or art.

In the early years of the 20th century, religion and semi-religion were quite popular in Beijing. Quietly, they entered the hearts of Beijingers. No commitment, vested with secular beauty, they enriched people's spiritual world and broadened their vistas, apart from their role as a kind of opium.

The duel pagodas in Qingshou Si (Longevity Celebration Temple) date back more than 800 years. They were pulled down in the 1950s to give way to the construction of a road.

Churches could be found everywhere in old Beijing. Beijingers called the churches in Bamiancao, Xuanwumen, Xizhimen and Xishiku districts the Eastern Church, Southern Church, Western Church and Northern Church respectively.

Praying Muslims in a mosque.

The Xishiku Church was originally located in Fuyou Street. When Ci Xi decided to build the western garden, she feared that people might spy on activities in the Zhongnanhai Garden from the high tower of the church. So negotiations were begun with the French owners of the church. Finally a large amount of silver and a lot of land were given to them to move the church to Xishiku, hence the Xishiku Church, which is the largest Catholic church in China.

Chapter 6
Temple Fairs and Theaters

Tianqiao in old Beijing became a place for folk artists towards the end of the Qing dynasty. There were all sorts of stalls and vendors selling bits and pieces, as well as snacks of all kinds.

Childhood Dreams

Temple fair at the East Temple.

The temple fair in Beijing was a show of popular culture of the old days. Locations for holding temple fairs in Beijing were rather scattered so that they were usually within walking distance of the local residents.

There were two types of temple fairs, regular and irregular. The former was held at a fixed time (for instance, a fixed date or two consecutive days in every ten days) and a fixed place. Peddlers had their fixed stalls too. The most representative temple fairs of such a fixed nature in the early 20th century were the fairs at the Eastern Temple and the Western Temple. The Eastern Temple referred to Longfu Si (Ample Fortune Temple) and the Western Temple Huguo Si (State Protection Temple). Besides, there were fairs at the White Dagoba Temple, Peach Palace, Dongyue Temple, etc. All in all, temple fairs were held every day in the city and peddlers would rush to those fairs from day to day. Temple fairs provided a means of life for and trained a large number of people such as folk artists, performers,

Temple fair taken in 1939 when Beijing was occupied by the Japanese invaders.

peddlers, etc. At the same time, they attracted huge numbers of visitors who came to entertain themselves. Annually there were irregularly-held fairs. such as the Changdian Temple Fair. It was located outside the Heping Gate. This temple fair was held from the first day to the fifth day of the first month of the Chinese New Year. On such an occasion, all other temple fairs were suspended. Peddlers would gather here. As the largest and most typical irregularly-held temple fair, Changdian Temple Fair had its unique characteristics and special commodities. Sweetened haws on bamboo sprigs that were as tall as a man and toy weathercocks made of corn stalks gave children everlasting memories. To go to the Changdian Temple Fair was a must for the New Year program of local residents. It was not rare for children living nearby to go to this fair three to five times during the New Year.

It is difficult to say if the activities in Tianqiao

Selling icicles and frozen foods that were kept in a cart, taken 60 years ago in Beijing.

Tianqiao provided all sorts of services such as fortune-telling, Qi Gong (breathing exercise), magic performances and ballad singing.

should also be regarded as a temple fair. In the area of Tianqiao, there were performances of local operas, acrobatics, juggling, minstrels, storytelling, songs and dances all year around. Internally, they were well organized, just like one might expect for a small closely knit community.

The temple fair was the epitome of local culture. It served as a supplement to the "cultural life of the main stream". Each adult citizen knew what he was doing in society and was happy to stay in that social stratum. Generally, this would remain unchanged. But this was not the case with a temple fair. There were all sorts of people coming to the temple fair to enjoy themselves. To go to a temple fair was different from going to a department store.

Though one might buy something at a temple fair, this was not the purpose a person had for visiting a temple fair. The person would not have a particular commodity in his mind and go straight to buy it. Instead, they would first wander around for a long time, comparing the same commodities at different stalls, striking up a conversation with sellers. Only when the person was satisfied, would he produce the money to buy an item. Deals at a temple fair were usually trifling. No one went to a temple fair to buy something urgently needed at home.

An antique connoisseur in Liulichang Street, which was known for selling curios, books and other cultural things. The eastern end of this street specialized in selling antiques.

Many a famous actors in Peking opera grew up at temple fairs. They would never forget the pleasant atmosphere at such fairs. Their appearance would cause a big stir and they would be followed by their fans. So they had to disguise themselves to avoid recognition. In this way, they could not only re-experience their childhood but also observe different people and their way of talking, which would be helpful to the portrayal of stage figures. One of

Paper of various sizes containing paintings or calligraphy hang in the street for sale. A vender might ask for a very high price, but you could bargain to reduce it.

A scene at Guan Ying Si (Avalokitesvara Temple).

hobbies of Mr. Wen Ouhong, a renowned playwright of Peking opera, was to go to temple fairs. Not only was he fond of temple fairs, he would often "grab" other people to go with him. Here is his description of going to Longfu Si Temple Fair together with famous Peking opera performer Gao Qingkui in 1935:

"The scale of Longfu Si Temple Fair tops all temple fairs in Beijing. The scope of the temple fair covers, apart from the three paths within the temple, Shenglu Street in front of the temple and two streets, the Eastern and Western Streets, at the southern end of Shenglu Street.

"On the northern side of Western Street around the corner of the Horse Market, there are rows of stalls under thick foliage, selling pets and birds. This is a specialized zone. The Eastern Street, linking Shenglu Street in the east, was lined with stalls selling miscellaneous items such as Qing-dynasty robes, coats, hats, decorative objects in floral patterns, court beads, fans, snuff bottles, antique bowls, hand-warming stoves, etc. This is also a specialized zone. Shenglu Street is a short street leading straight to the front gate of the temple.

Mr. Wen Ouhong, a renowned playwright of Peking operas and an opera critic.

A store hung up a canvas to keep out the sun so that it could do business.

People milling around at Longfu Si (Ample Fortune Temple).

Among some meat shops in this street there is a store selling cases made of lacquer with engraved patterns, and a roomy House of Birds, in front of which stands a high rack hanging with various bird cages. Here you may find myna, hill myna, and colorful parrots which could imitate human speech. Then, divided by species, there are cages of various birds. Spread on the ground

An elderly man teasing his bird.

are plumes of peacocks, golden pheasants, black bone chickens and so on. Sometimes there are also apes, tigers, squirrels, etc., for the rich customers. The owner of the House of Birds is a woman who often sits on a bench leisurely smoking a long pipe and serving customers.

"The main ground of Longfu Si has three pathways. When you enter the main entrance and follow the central pathway, you would come to the ruins of a Buddhist hall. Here there is a large but neat market. Displayed on the first level which is close to the entrance are things like baskets, dustpans, chicken feather dusters, steamers, washing boards. On the levels behind it are places for performances. In between those performing arenas are stalls selling douzhier, a fermented drink made from ground beans, pig head meat, bean curd with sauce, cakes, pan-fried sausage, broth, etc. On the final level there are fortunetellers, palm readers, venders selling foreign cigarette pictures, clay figurine molds, etc.

At a temple fair, between the stalls selling snacks, were performers of opera, comic dialogues, juggling, and so on.

A Taoist enjoying a snack at the Tianqiao Temple Fair.

The sweet smell of the food stall attracted dogs too.

"On the western pathway, as soon as you enter the gate, you will see a stall selling rice cakes. Next to it is an arena selling golden fish. To go further north along this pathway you would come to several fairly large stalls selling 'antiques'. There are a few stalls selling unique articles. One is specialized in shuttlecocks. Shuttlecocks are divided into three types, the best one being the feather shuttlecock. One stall sells string holders of Chinese fiddles. They are carved bone or ivory and bamboo, looking most exquisite and refined. Another stall sells something called 'cotton cats'. Cotton is used to make cats and dogs to be

Vendors were expecting customers to buy their congee, wine, or sprigs of sugared haw.

pasted on a piece of paper. It is rather fun. Another sells snuff bottles with pictures painted inside. Apart from ordinary figurines, there are stage scenes of Peking operas. One could even recognize the renowned actor Tan Xingpei in costume.

"That day Gao Qingkui and I just sauntered at the temple fair; we had no intention of buying flowers or birds. We just entered the Eastern Street. Before long, we heard the rhythmic clinking sound of tapping on some bronze tea service plate. 'Here's the first stop,' I said to myself. In front of us was a two-meter long stall. There were a few glass cases in which stood several figurines in costumes on a piece of blue cloth. There were generals, officials and others imitating stage scenes from some Peking opera. On a tiny piece of wooden board there were written names. The head of such a figurine was made of clay while the body made of pulp. It was then decorated with colorful paper and costumes. It had no feet because a circle of bristle was neatly stuck around its waist, hence the name 'bristle

Paper-cutting was another popular folk art in old Beijing.

Children were fascinated by the maker of figurines in the shadow play.

figurine'. In front of the stall, I showed them to Mr. Gao. He marveled at the craftsmanship of the figurine sculptures which were so faithful to the stage figures. 'The first stop of yours is very interesting,' he said. 'Obviously it is not without reason because of your love of operas.'

We walked a few more steps and came to the second stop - a stall of shadow play figures. This stall was tiny, a table with a simple, three-tier rack standing on it. On this rack there were shadow play figures. They were only samples. The owner's real stuff was wrapped in a piece of blue cloth beneath the table. The shadow play figures were flat and thin, which could be kept in an album. In his blue bag there were a dozen such albums. Each album kept 'body', 'head', 'cart and horse', 'bird and beast', 'knife and spear', 'table and chair'. This bag of his was as good as a box of complete stage sets.

Wen Kui Tang was a bookstore with a long history. This was taken in 1939.

Mr. Gao was delighted. When I told the stall owner the name of Mr. Gao, he immediately held his hands in front of his chest and said with elation, 'I've been looking forward to meeting you, sir. It's my great pleasure that you've come. I hope you would condescend to give me some instructions.' So saying, he rummaged through his bag under the table and fished out some 'heads' from an album at the bottom of the pile and showed them to Mr. Gao.

"Mr. Gao cried in surprise, 'Ah, this is Old Tan (Tan Zhi in the role of General Huang Zhong in *Ding Jun Shan*)! This is Big Head (Wang Guifeng in the role of Liu Zhang in Rang Chengdu)!'"

Then Mr. Wen and Mr. Gao came to their third stop - the stall of "dough figurines of Tang". Master Tang was one of the most famous craftsmen at the time. The craftsmanship of making figurines with dough had been handed down for generations in the Tang family. During its heyday, there were several renowned craftsmen in one generation. Mr. Wen was quite familiar with the Tangs. Master Tang asked Wen and Gao to make dramatic poses on the spot. They complied. Master Tang gazed at them for a second and then turned to his dough. In a short moment he produced two lifelike dough figurines imitating Wen and Gao. Finally he gave them to Gao for a keepsake.

A scene from the film "Amusing Marriage", starred with Zheng Xiaoqiu and Hu Die. The story took place in Beijing.

Theater, Opera Stars and Fans

Now let's move to the theater that was also one of the principal characteristics of Beijing. If you came to Beijing for a visit you would have to go to the theater to watch Peking opera once or twice. Otherwise, you would miss the best part of the city. The most influential local opera in Beijing was Peking opera. In the old days, theaters were mostly located on both sides of Qianmenwai Avenue. By the early 20th century, there were a dozen theaters there. Later on, theaters began to be built in the inner city. The most renowned ones were Xin Xin, Chang'an, Jixiang, and Haerfei. Since these were built later, they had more attractive architecture and had better acoustics. The performing style was relatively new. If you went to the old theaters like Guanghe, Guangde or Huale in Qianmenwai Avenue, you would have operas mostly in old music.

Here is an old photo showing a stage scene of *Putting the Son to Death* at Yuanmen. The performer in the role of the heroine, Mu Guiyin, is obviously a

Performers in the Peking opera *Put the Son to Death* at Yuanmen had their picture taken in this photo studio.

Children were fond of the Monkey King but panicked when seeing the Painted Face in a Peking opera.

Some 60 or 70 years ago, people sat on three sides of a stage in Beijing theaters. While a Peking opera was being performed, attendants walked around in the theater pouring tea, offering towels or even selling cigarettes and melon seeds.

man. I suppose he must have been quite well known at the time. What is amusing is the little boy standing before the chair. He had to act the role of Yang Zongbao, fiancé of Mu Guiyin. Their ages are out of proportion. However, Mu Guiyin is still very earnest in striking a pose.

Another photo shows a stage and some actors. The inscription on this photo is "Beijing Theater". But which theater was this? I asked an elderly man and he said that it was probably the Kaiming Theater. The actors are all children in costume. Before the normal size of the table and chairs, they look even smaller. On the one side of the exit, there is a signboard with such words: "Tan Fuying staring in the *Nanyang Pass* and *Knocking off the Tablet*. They are probably the titles of the next day's program. The stage is edged with a low railing. Beyond the railing lay some tables covered with tea pots and cups, plates of melon seeds, etc. The audience sitting in front must have bought them on the spot. While watching an opera, they did not forget to nibble something. Occasionally they had to clap. Don't you think they were rather busy?

Mr. Mei Lanfang, a famous Peking opera actor, played the role of a heroine in *Life and Death Hatred* in 1935.

Here is a photo of the famous actor Mei Lanfang in the opera *Life and Death Hatred*. This photo was taken when he was in his heyday as an actor. Unfortunately it is only a portrait of his upper body, a close-up. If only it were a picture of his whole body you could easily imagine his gracefulness in acting and would find him fascinating. It was the time for Peking opera. Mei Lanfang, Shang Xiaoyun, Cheng Yanqiu and Xun Huisheng were regarded as the best four *dan* performers. Then there were four best *xu sheng* performers, four best junior *dan* performers, and four best *kun dan* performers, as well as the four best *dan* performers of Shanghai. Even the role of "Painted Face", which had been long neglected, had the so-called "three best heroes", namely, Jin Shaoshan, Hao Shouchen and Hou Xirui.

Clowns, the most insignificant role of all in Peking opera, had renowned representatives such as Xiao Changhua, Ye Shengzhang and Ma Fulu. Peking opera was no longer limited in Beijing alone. In Shanghai

Above the curtain of a door on the left side of the stage, there were two characters, "chu jiang", "entering" through which performers entered the stage. On the right, there were "ru xiang¡" above another curtained door, meaning "exit" through which performers left the stage.

Puppet shows were often performed in serial form.

there was the famous Shanghai School headed by Zhou Xingfang and Gai Jiaotian. Peking opera became very popular in Beijing and Shanghai. An actor had to be hailed in both cities to be considered a star. Those who were less well known made the city of Tianjin their springboard. Apart from those three cities, Peking opera grew popular also in cities such as Nanjing, Wuhan, Shenyang and Xi'an. Naturally it was appropriate to call Peking opera the national opera.

In those days, an actor needed

Changyin Ge (Resonant Voice Pavilion) was a large stage in the Forbidden City. It had three floors and a performance could be staged on each floor to indicate what was happening simultaneously in Heaven, on earth, and in the nether world. It was known as one the Three Great Stages, the other two being De He Yuan (Garden of Moral Harmony) in the Summer Palace and Qingyin Ge (Clear Voice Pavilion) at the summer resort of Chengde.

Jing Yun Da Gu, a kind of ballad singing rhymed to the beat of a drum, was very popular for a time in Beijing. It spawned a number of good performers.

to have his own following in order to be a star. Whenever he was going to perform, his fans would come despite rain and wind. Both the actor and his fans were of the same age group. When the actor was an apprentice, his later fans would have been children too. By the time he began to appear on stage, those children had become grown-ups and would come to applaud him.

When talking about the prosperity of Peking opera, we need to mention Empress Dowager Ci Xi. The name of Ci Xi cannot be avoided in discussing the role of Peking opera in Chinese history. She was a great lover of Peking opera, and she gathered almost all the good actors of Peking opera and kept them for the imperial house. The actors regarded it as a great honor to be selected to perform for the Qing Court. Their performances pleased the Qing Court and they themselves learned about the life of those high-ranking officials there. Later, when they performed in roles of high-ranking officials, they certainly knew how to act. Actors

like Tan Xinpei, Yang Xiaolou, Shang Xiaoyun were all able to learn what they needed from those high-ranking officials they saw.

This most precious photo shows Mei Lanfang, Wang Youqing (right) and Wang Shaoqing (left), all practitioners of Peking opera, at the residence of Feng Guozhang in Beijing in 1913.

Hollywood films began to enter China during the 1930s. The photo shows an advertisement for an American film in a Beijing street.

A cinema at Tianqiao of Beijing.

A girls' choir at a girls' school in 1940s.

A singing performance staged by a school in Beijing. The musical instrument was the dulcimer, which was very popular at that time.

Lamentation

Yang Xiaolou, a famous Peking opera actor, died in 1938. The funeral in his honor was extremely pompous. The following is a descriptive record of the funeral written by Ding Binsui, late drama critic of Taiwan.

The funeral was most elaborate. The brand-new sedan-chair housing the coffin was carried by 64 people. What was most particular about it was that a man nicknamed "A Tuft of Hairs" was employed to toss the paper money. As was local custom in Beijing, a man would go along with the coffin while tossing paper money on the way to the grave. What was important was that he must have the ability to toss it high and far away. The chap had a mole with some hairs on his cheek, hence the nickname. His true name was forgotten. He had done this since he was a child and now he was really an expert in such a mission. Having been engaged in tossing paper money for scores of years, he had names for various ways of tossing. For

Paper coins danced in midair as a funeral procession passed.

instance, tossing paper money high in midair and letting it fall straight was called "a caw that shakes Heaven"; tossing it not so high but in a scattered manner was called "a sky of stars". The man had retired after long years of service. Now he was invited to toss paper money again and was promised a high pay. Since it was for Yang Xiaolou, he was eager to render his service, too. Sure enough, he did a good job. There were many idlers in Beijing, who were enthusiastic about anything exciting. On learning "A Tuft of Hairs" would toss paper money, they crowded streets to enjoy the fun. Besides, Beijing teemed with fans of Peking opera. However, they could rarely see the renowned

A pine-made lion in a funeral procession.

actors themselves. Yang Xiaolou was the greatest master of Peking opera of the time and the late chairman of the Peking Opera Guild. All the famous actors, managers and attendants in this line attended the funeral. So it was indeed a parade of Peking opera performers in plain clothes, besides his relatives. Peking opera fans would not miss such an opportunity. In threes and fives, they stood looking on and tried to seek out some renowned figures. They chatted animatedly, pointing to some familiar faces. Take Xiao Cuihua for example. He was in a pale-pinkish-greg robe, two large black eyes on his dark face darted here and there. He held some joss-sticks in one hand and a purple handkerchief in the other. Whenever he came across someone familiar, he would smile a smile with the handkerchief over his mouth. Such scenes were not easy to see. Naturally opera fans vied with one another to see those stars in the street.

This funeral had a great impact on the society. In the past, actors of Peking opera had fascinated numerous fans with their stage art. After the anti-Japanese war broke out, Mei Lanfang, Chen Yanqiu, and others left the stage one after another. Stages of Peking opera in Beiping became rather desolate. To the disappointment of Beijingers, Master Yang passed away. The grand funeral was, in a way, a lament to the decline of Peking opera.

Peking opera was, of course, just one of the Chinese local operas. But it was not simply a form of performing arts. Internally, it was semi-religious. Anyone who started learning Peking opera as a small boy had to simultaneously accept a relation to a particular school and another relation to a particular clan. The two relationships would be his support for the rest of his life.

A lecture in a drama school. This school was founded in 1930.

Both the school and the clan expanded. As time went on, one would grow stronger than the other or vice versa. This promoted a semi-religious atmosphere. By "semi-religious", I mean it was somewhat similar to a religion. In the early days, such practices were helpful to the survival of Peking opera and the development of its art. But later, its negative effect began to show and grow.

Portraits of Mei Lanfang, Shang Xiaoyun, Chen Yanqiu and Xun Huisheng, all of whom excelled in female roles. They were the most famous four actors of Peking opera.

Chapter 7
Subordinates of the Capital

The leisurely life in old Beijing was kaleidoscopic. People of different classes had different customs and ways of life.

Minced Sheep Offal and Salty Pepper

A flower lover in Beijing.

In this large city of Beijing lived the emperor, his officials, and the common folk under their rule. Though they existed under the same blue sky and on the same piece of land, there was nothing in common between them as far as life was concerned. The common folk, living at the bottom of the social stratum, were merely slaves of the imperial house and the officials. They did sometimes resist, but at the same time they grew apathetic and numb. Endurance of hardship, mere existence, and living a befuddled life was their common experience. Negative attitudes were in control of many ordinary people's minds. Even officials who fell into disfavor were more or less affected. In the labyrinth of crisscrossed hutongs outside the Qianmen Gate, there were all sorts of renowned stores, pompous and full of commotion. The social setting was ordered to satisfy people's carnal desires and make them forget about the misery and grief of society. This probably served as a basis for the common folk's culture in

Beijing.

Life in Beijing was leisurely and comfortable, and rich in variety. However, everything had its own place. The norms could not be disrupted. A dinner at the New Year's Eve, firecrackers on the Spring Festival day, meat dumplings on the fifth day of the first month, sweet dumplings on the fifteenth day of the first month. Each of these came in good order.

As for flowers, there were peach blossoms in spring, lotus in summer, chrysanthemum in autumn and plum blossoms in winter. As for food, one could eat at home or eat out; one could have a simple meal or have a grand dinner. It would usually be better to have a simple meal at home. Ingredients for a dish were about the same whether at home or in a restaurant. The cooking methods were similar too, be they for chicken or fish. Vegetables were handy. Everybody knew how to prepare them. The only difference between cooking in a restaurant and at home was that the latter followed

Some read classic works in order to climb up the social ladder, others sought stimulus by smoking opium. They were all Beijingers.

rules that were not as strict as the former in terms of the preparation of ingredients and cooking methods. But there was a world of difference in cost. If one fancied a grand dinner, one had to say what kind of restaurant they wanted to go to and what cuisine they wanted to taste.

In the early years of the Republic, there were the "Great Eight", all specializing in Shandong cuisine. Later on, Peking duck became popular. It first appeared as duck roasted in an oven at the Bianyifang Restaurant. Then there was the Quanjude Restaurant's duck that was hung up to be roasted. After that, the instant boiled mutton of Donglaishun Restaurant began to become popular among Beijingers. Then there appeared a number of good cuisines such as the "Four Great Cuisines" or the "Eight Great Cuisines", all coming from other parts of the country.

Women having a picture taken in a park. This was another way to enjoy life in old Beijing.

Let's now move to the Beijingers' apparel. In winter, there was cotton, leather and silk floss clothing. In summer, there was silk, satin and damask silk. In the good seasons of spring and autumn, there were all sorts of materials and styles available to wear.

As for drinks, would one prefer liquor or tea? One could sip a cup of liquor on his own or booze up with friends. If that was not enough, one could play finger games to determine who would pay for the drinks. In earlier times, those rolling in money feared drinking alone and would engage prostitutes or homosexuals for company. As for tea, one could have either green tea or jasmine tea.

A teahouse.

Beijingers were fond of jasmine tea, though they were well aware that people in the South drank green tea. One might find a quiet place at home, pour oneself a pot of tea and sit sipping it while enjoying the view of a pot of chrysanthemums. In the streets, there were plenty of teahouses. There were several kinds. In certain teahouses, tea was the only thing available. In others, one might enjoy a performance of *ping shu* and *da gu* while drinking tea; or one might order a simple meal or some snacks; or one could even play chess.

Those who were strong earned a living by doing heavy manual work. The saying was: "those who work with their brains rule and those who work with their brawn are ruled." But who were those who "worked with their brains?" They included officials, merchants, teachers, journalists, writers, etc. Though they could be classified into many categories, their number was small. As for manual laborers, there was no limit in number available. In the streets, there were rickshaw boys, tricycle boys, coal briquette makers, etc. There were too many categories to name.

It was sons and daughters of the "Eight Banners of Manchu", rulers of China, who began to smoke opium in north China. There was a couplet that made the point regarding the harm of opium: "A pipe that kills all heroes without a stain of blood; a little light that burns down all the buildings without slight ash."

A prostitute and her customer in old Beijing.

Three opium addicts, all bags of bones, on a street corner.

Photo of a fashionable girl of Beijing in late Qing dynasty.

Fashionable women on a Beijing street. Permed hair, high-heeled leather shoes and *qi bao* (dress in Manchurian style) with high slits on the sides began to appear in the 1930s and 1940s.

Clothes, Food, Housing and Traffic

Now I would like to talk about Beijingers' clothes, food, housing and traffic.

Clothes: Beijing was very strict about etiquette. A city of different classes, strata and nationalities, there was a good basis for the existence of such etiquette. One typical example was how Pu Yi treated his younger brother after he had become the emperor. Pu Yi was only ten years old when he assumed the throne. One day, when he met his younger brother Pu Jie who was about five or six years old, he flared up with his eyes wide open, demanding all of a sudden, "Are you qualified to wear this robe?" Pu Jie lowered his head to look at his robe. It was an ordinary robe embroidered with a dragon that had four talons. That should not be an issue, he thought. An emperor could wear the robe embroidered with a dragon with five talons. His dragon only had four talons. He did not do anything wrong. As he was wondering what the matter was, Pu Yi said, "I mean the color!" Now Pu Jie realized that he was

A Han family of the early Republic. Their attire was obviously influenced by the Manchu style of clothing.

Mother and son dressed in Manchurian style clothing at the end of the Qing dynasty.

mistakenly wearing a bright yellow robe which was used only by the emperor. He apologized immediately. Generally speaking, officials put on their official garments on formal occasions. Privately, they wore casual clothing. This was a flexible "iron rule". On formal occasions, for example, Yuan Shikai and his generals wore army uniforms with a feather adorning each hat and decorative objects all over their bodies. But privately they preferred a robe and a coat. At that time, a boy student had a robe when going out while a girl student wore a white or light-colored blouse and a black skirt, as well as a pair of knee-high socks and cloth-made shoes with a strap for fastening over the upper part of the foot.

It was a vogue to have a "cherry mouth". The three women in the photo all had little red-lipped mouths.

Typical clothes for men, women, and children during the Qing dynasty.

Young men and women of the Republic. Men usually wore a cap and women liked to sport fringes on their foreheads.

Ladies with fringes during the Republic.

After the "May the Fourth Movement" of 1919, Western suits began to appear. When Sun Yat-sen became president, the Yat-sen suit became popular. For women, the *qi pao* was in vogue.

There were also clothes for special occasions such as "wedding dresses" and "funeral dresses". There were differences in dress from nationality to nationality, from class to class. The Han people's clothes could be very different from those of the Manchurian people. There also existed difference in their cultures.

Food: The food of the Han people and the Manchurian people was different too. The Manchurian people were fond of roasted meat, while the

Sleeveless *qi bao* revealed the curved line of a woman's figure. The three portraits of females were printed on calendars of 1930s to 1940s in Shanghai. They were models of that time.

A fully dressed-up bride of a Han family with a "Phoenix Crown" on her head, a colorful brocade draped on her shoulders, and a silk flower adorning her chest.

Han people liked to cook. Later on, they gradually merged these preferences and as a result there appeared the Grand Banquet of Manchu and Han. Such a banquet was said to be held only on grand occasions and would last for three consecutive days. Food provided for such a banquet is available today in Fang Shan Restaurant in Beihai Park. However, people of today cannot afford such a long time for a meal. So the so-called Grand Banquet of Manchu and Han today is only a selection of dishes from the old menu. What is also worth mentioning is the wonderful Beijing snacks. Douzhier, for instance, was something indispensable to many old

A bridegroom normally wore a long gown and a felt hat with a red flower on his chest.

Beijingers, but totally unacceptable to people outside Beijing. It is made of the bean starch used for making vermicelli. When the dregs sink and are removed, the liquid is poured into a large vat to be fermented. The snack is ready to serve once it is heated. To go with this drink, there are hot pickles, roasted pancakes and *jiaoquan*, a deep-fried crisp dough in the shape of a doughnut. Such snacks are inexpensive but delicious. What's more, they help the digestion. Some seventy or eighty years ago, restaurants in Beijing were almost all dominated by Shandong cuisine. Sea food

Douzhier, a fermented drink made of ground beans, was unpalatable to people out of Beijing, but a delight to local residents.

Dongxinglou Restaurant, located on busy Donghuamen Street, was known for its fish.

The grand fa?ade of the Jixiantang Restaurant in Beijing at that time.

Peking duck.

came from the sea coast of Shandong. The chefs also came from Shandong. It was not until the 40s of 20th century that Peking duck and instant boiled mutton rose in popularity, surpassing Shandong cuisine. Later on, eight different cuisines entered Beijing. Thus the dominant position of Shandong cuisine in Beijing came to an end.

Housing: Housing for the different classes of people was quite different. The Imperial Palace was used by the imperial house. Residences of princes and the emperor's brothers were called *wang fu* (prince mansions). Residences of crown princes, *bei le*, *bei*

An elaborately-built wall of a prince's mansion.

zi; residences of Lord of State Security, and Lord of State in Assistance to the Emperor were called *fu* (mansion). There were strict rules regarding the number of rooms, colors, pictures, height of the base, and number of nails on the gate to the mansions of different rankings. If one violated such rule by using something permitted for those above one's ranking, this would be regarded as having committed a crime and one would be beheaded. Below these were the ministers, *da xue shi*, and ministers of *jun ji chu*. Such residences could not be called *fu*, no matter how grand they might be. Further down were the wealthy people. They had to be very careful when

A man who migrated from south China to Beijing would keep something southern in his residence.

living in Beijing. If one did something that breached the rules, that person would probably be reported and punished. His property would then be confiscated. This was a way of keeping balance between power and wealth.

Due to the cold climate, Beijingers, compared with those who lived in the South, gave much more attention to their houses being airtight and solid enough to keep in the warmth. This was true for both the Imperial Palace and ordinary people's *siheyuan* residences.

Traffic: Obvious improvements have been made in the means of transportation. People of today probably would not believe that boats were once a common means of transport in Beijing. In the south of the city

A school converted from a Qing-dynasty prince's mansion during the time of Republic.

Bedroom of a late Qing-dynasty residence.

once existed a network of waterways. A small river to the east of the Qianmen Gate flowed towards the southeast. In fact there were several rivers in Beijing at that time. In the Xicheng (western city) District, a river ran from south to north. Even today, the area where the White Dagoba stands is called the "riverside".

A well-off family.

Before the Heping Gate was built, there had existed a river from Liubukou to Hufangqiao. In the Dongcheng (eastern city) District, there once flowed a river that passed where the Beijing Railway Station now stands. The moat around the city was rather wide. From some old photos we can see boats sailing in the moat. But on

City wall at Chaoyang Gate, the moat and the ferry boats.

the whole, compared with the southern part of the country, Beijing had fewer rivers. Transport by land was dominant.

At first, there were only carts, horses, sedan-chairs, etc. The carts included wheelbarrows, flat-board carts, horse carts, donkey carts, etc. The wheelbarrow, which was commonly used for the transport of goods and people in the suburbs, no longer exists. The rickshaw (locally known as *huang bao che, jiao pi, che zai,* respectively) originated in Japan and grew to be very popular in Shanghai, Tianjin and Guangzhou. After the rickshaw, there were pedicabs that could be seen everywhere in Beijing in

those days. Some could carry only one passenger, others could carry two. A good pedicab had a canopy over it to keep out the sun. In winter, passengers would be given a blanket to cover their legs for warmth. There was charter service, too, for the rich. The very rich even began to purchase cars. For a long period of time, the imperial house refused to have one. The reason they refused seems to our ears ridiculous. They simply could not tolerate a driver sitting at the front of the car. So it was some VIPs working in the government and army, and two Peking opera performers, Mei Lanfang and Shang Xiaoyun, who were the first to use cars in Beijing.

A rickshaw and a wheelbarrow.

The first motor vehicle for public transport was the tram, which was then followed by the bus. There were only a few bus routes at first. Gradually the whole city was crisscrossed by routes. Then those bus routes expanded to the outskirts of the city. Train service was barred by the city wall. Both the Emperor and the common people would not accept the idea of breaking the city wall in order to let the train through. The Emperor

Animals used as a means of transport could be dated back to ancient days.

Waiting for customers.

An old-fashioned motor vehicle made in Europe and driven on a Beijing street.

feared that the "imperial air" might leak out if the city wall was broken open, and that would shake the rule of the Emperor over the whole country. As for the commoners, they were quite frightened to see such a huge moving monster that spit steam. But several years later, the train entered the city after all, and the Eight Allied Forces entered Beijing by train. Empress Dowager Ci Xi did not take the train to flee Beijing. But when she returned, she did ride in a train to enter Beijing. The Qianmen Railway Station was one of the earliest railway stations built in China. It was a makeshift station at first, just for the purpose of transporting troops and goods after the

A tram in Beijing in the 1930s.

invasion of Beijing by the Eight Allied Forces. That is why the station was built in a place so close to the Dongjiao Minxiang legation. It was then used for half a century.

Cultural relics and antiques were most popular among Beijingers. It is said that there are two reasons: One, some cultural relics and antiques were scattered among people after the looting of Yuan Ming Yuan (Garden of Perfection and Brightness) and the Imperial Palace, etc. Two, many Qing-dynasty nobles and officials, who were down and out, had to sell their cultural relics and antiques in order to make a living. Because of this, there appeared a large number of collectors, connoisseurs and curio dealers. The photo shows a metal and stone expert carving a piece of stone.

Beijingers of the Past Seen in Photos

A joyful trumpeter.

Let's have a look at a few old photos.

This is a trumpet blower in a wedding procession, wearing a rich and inscrutable expression. He was obviously enjoying his own skill rather than offering congratulations to the newly-wedded.

This photo shows a display of odds and ends for sale. Though most had little value, the vendor cleaned each piece until it was spotless. While cleaning each object, he tried to make up a story about it. When someone showed some interest in an object, even if it was only a glance at it, the vendor would tell a story about the object and the customer might then willingly buy it, paying quite a sum.

The vendor in this photo is a Muslim. Muslim people in Beijing were known for their love of cleanliness. Just look at him, he was making everything shine so that it would naturally attract customers.

Let's try to figure out the mentality of the puppet

Kerosene stoves, tin wine pots, porcelain soap boxes, and old spectacles¡- were all cleaned spotless.

How much could a skein of yarn fetch? Though the profit was little, the vendor was enthusiastic in hawking his wares.

A Muslim vendor selling food cleaned all his pots until they were bright and shining.

player hidden behind the worn-out cloth curtain. He had no idea of the size of his audience, nor if they could afford to offer him any coins. However, with great earnestness, he manipulated the puppets while singing or speaking for them. The money he earned after a whole day's hard work might not even earn him a square meal. But for the time being, he was totally engrossed in the performance.

This man was creating figurines by blowing air into a piece of melted sugar. Squatting leisurely at the foot of a wall, he made figurines of birds, butterflies, knives, and rifles, all of which were laid

out on a rack to be displayed. Unfortunately, we can not see how they were made. There must have been a crowd of children watching him pick up melted sugar from a little heated stove and turning it into something lively by blowing on it and sculpturing it. The money he earned after a whole day's hard work might not even earn him a square meal. But for the time being, he was totally engrossed in the performance. The latter, to him, was more

A puppet show that attracted both adults and children.

important, for he enjoyed in such creation of beauty. If he argued for each cent for his ware, he might not be able to live on in case the money he was able to get was too little.

Beijingers often idled away their time by kicking shuttlecocks, keeping birds, flying kites, etc. This photo shows a man working on a piece of embroidery. To him, this was no game at all. Once he completed it, what he felt, I imagine, would be pride and satisfaction.

Most Beijingers were optimistic about life. Optimism helped them deal with all sorts of embarrassments caused by poverty.

Beating his gong to sell candies.

Boy selling kites and an elderly man working on his embroidery.

Among the archives of the old photos, there are a few valuable but shocking ones showing people being beheaded.

During the Ming dynasty (1368-1644), the execution ground was near Xisi Pailou. It was later moved to Caishikou. This remained unchanged until the Qing dynasty (1644-1911). Death sentences were carried out shortly before the Winter Solstice every year. So this time was also known as the "Autumn Execution". Before the verdict of death was handed down, a suspect had to go through a final hearing that was known as a "Court Trial", at which he would

A bird fancier.

A courteous contest of chess.

be sentenced either to death or temporary suspension of the execution sentence. Those who got the death sentence would be carted back to prison. On such occasions, the streets on which the carts would pass would be heavily guarded, not allowing ordinary people to watch. Those who got temporary suspension of execution would be carted to the prisons of the Board of Punishment. There was no cloth covering such carts. Relatives and friends of those convicts would come and wait for results, holding rings of haw in their hands. When the carts passed, they would swarm the procession of the carts and look for their dear ones cart by cart. Once they found them, they would rush up shouting, "Great fortune has fallen on you!" At the same time, they would put the rings of haw around the person's neck. The convict would reply, "Thank you!"

A death sentence would have to be approved by the Emperor. The day before the execution, prison wardens would say to the convict, "Great fortune has fallen on you!" The convict understood immediately that he would be executed the next day. That night, servants would be sent to wash his face, comb his hair and help him put on new clothes provided by his family. Each convict would be given, by the prison authorities, a catty of pancakes and a package of braised meat. If his family was wealthy, he would be allowed to have a square meal sent in by his family. At daybreak the next day, such convicts would be taken out of their cells and trussed up. Then a roll call would be carried out. They would be carted to Caishikou to be executed. The carts stopped at a wine shop known as the "Broken Bowl" on the east side of the Xuanwu Gate Outer Avenue. The convicts were there offered a mixture of rice wine and alcohol, which was very strong. After a convict downed a bowl of such drink, an escort would toss the bowl away, breaking it at once. This was how the wine shop got such a name. At that time, no other wine shops in Beijing dared use chipped bowls to sell wine or liquor. If they did, customers would not only refuse to pay but also swear at the shop owners. If this happened to a wine shop, its owner would have to lump it. The convicts, already dead drunk, would continue their trip to the execution ground. There were three executioners to carry out each execution. One would put an iron device around the neck of the convict, and another hold tight the trussing-up behind the convict. At the moment when the former pulled the iron device forward and the latter pulled the rope backward, the third executioner would cut the convict's head off with a long knife.

At the Caishikou execution ground, robbers, corrupted officials, and vicious persons were put to death. However, records show that some innocent and righteous people, who had been framed, were also beheaded there. Two renowned generals of the Ming dynasty (1368-1644) who achieved great merit in border battles were wrongly put to death at Caishikou at the order of a fatuous and self-indulgent emperor. Su Shun and seven other high-ranking officials who had been entrusted by the late Emperor to assist the new Emperor were executed at Caishikou, too, because of opposi-

Scene of the execution ground.

Scene of a Japanese solder of the Eight Allied Forces cleaning his saber after killing one of the Boxers.

tion to Empress Dowager Ci Xi. In 1898 when the Reform Movement failed, famous reformists known as the "Six Gentlemen", including Tan Sitong, Lin Xu, and Yang Rui, were killed at Caishikou on the order of Ci Xi. In 1898 when the Reform Movement failed, famous reformists known as the "Six Gentlemen", including Tan Sitong, Lin Xu and Yang Rui, were killed at Caishikou on the order of Ci Xi. A large number of reformists were arrested. According to historical records, Tan Sitong and Liang Qichao went to the Japanese embassy and met an attaché. Tan wrote for the attaché to read, "Mr. Liang must not die and will be most useful in future. I hope you will do some justice." The attaché consented and wrote, "You may also stay here, sir, to keep out of danger."

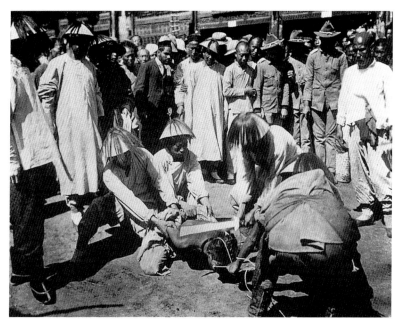

The Qing troops executed one of the Boxers under the supervision of foreign solders.

Tan shook his head and wrote, "If this gentleman is unable to escape, we would have no one for the future. If I am not to die, I would let down our forerunners. Chen Ying's pestle and mortar, each has its own function."

Chapter 8
A Picture of Secular Life

This is a painting of a hat shop probably in Dashanlan. The owner, the customers, attendants and a monk begging for food, are all vivid and lifelike. It was executed by a foreign artist who was obviously quite familiar with life in old Beijing.

A Place of Significant Events

What is superb about Beijing is its cultural scene. Such a scene can be divided into two categories. One refers to the highbrow culture that was mostly shown through the imperial culture in the past. The other refers to community culture, or the commoners' culture. Each had its own advantages. But on many occasions they were opposed to each other, or sometimes, were supplementary to each other.

The former is seen towards the end of the Qing dynasty (1644-1911), for example, in the "Gong Che Petition", Tan Sitong being beheaded at Caishikou, the burning down of the Zhao family building during the May 4th Movement, Liu Hezheng being killed in front of the building of the Duan Qirui government. In modern times, one good example comes in the people's response to the death of Sun Yat-sen. When he passed away in Beijing and the coffin was laid in the Yat-sen Park for a few days, some 740,000 people went there to pay homage and watched in respect when the hearse moved to Biyun Si (Temple of Azure Clouds). Four years

Boating on Kunming Lake.

In the early 1920s, the Ming Tombs were the targets of looters. A great deal of earth was carted away and stone stele on the Sacred Way leading to the tombs was much damaged.

later when the coffin was moved to the Yat-sen Mausoleum in Nanjing, Beijingers again turned out to see him off. Many precious photos recording these events have been handed down. Beijing is a city that has seen many significant political and military events. In my opinion, oil paintings should be made on the basis of those photos. The oil paintings, if done, would place Beijing high above other cities.

But the community culture of Beijing is somewhat less glamorous. As soon as "old Beijing" is mentioned, it immediately reminds people of the secular life of the people living at the bottom of society. They not only make our hearts warm but provide us much to relish. They could be more touching than political and military events. I do not know the reason for this. Perhaps, there have been too many examples of the imperial events in the past century and people are just fed

The Seventeen-arch Bridge in the Summer Palace.

up with them.

Let's now leaf through photos showing scenes of weddings and funerals in 'Old Beijing. Talking of weddings and funerals, there were numerous rituals and rules. Take marriage for instance. Parents on both sides would have to check the hours when the bride and bridegroom were born and see if these did not clash with each other. Then the betrothal gifts had to be prepared by the parents of the bridegroom and delivered to the home of the bride. After that a date would be fixed for the wedding ceremony (including sending a sedan chair to carry the bride; the kowtowing to each other by the two to be wedded; a grand dinner, etc.). A fortnight later, the new couple would visit the parents of the bride. Each of these events had its rules. Here I would like to cite the example of a typical wedding ceremony of Manchurians.

Before the sedan chair set off to carry the bride, gongs and drums would sound in front of the bridegroom's house for a long time. An eternal light would be lit. A bed would be fully prepared. A procession of sedan chairs carrying the bridegroom and other important figures would head for the bride's home amidst the sound of drums and gongs. When they arrived, they would find the gate to the bride's house shut. So the ceremony master would have to knock on the door ask-

Photo of Cao Rulin, Zhang Zongxiang and other leading members of the Beiyang Government taken in the Central Park of Beijing. In 1919, Cao, Zhang and Lu Zongyu acted to sell out China at the Paris Peace Conference and this ignited the May Fourth Movement, which soon spread all over the country and marked a milestone of the Chinese revolution.

An archway was set up in front of the Tiananmen to celebrate the fall of the Qing dynasty and the founding of the Republic.

Sun Yat-sen memorial hall in the Yat-sen Park.

Tiananmen
(northern side)

People of Beijing gathered to celebrate the success of the Northern Expedition.

Beijing fell to the Japanese invaders in the summer of 1937. Chinese students were then forced to participate in a demonstration against Britain.

Student demonstration on a Beijing street in the 1930s.

Group wedding ceremonies became popular during the 1930s to 1940s. This is an old photo of a "new development" of the time.

ing for admittance. As trumpeters and drummers employed by the bride's side played their musical instruments, the bride would begin to make final touches to her wedding dress and make-up.

When the gate was opened, all guests would enter the house of the bride. A banquet would be spread out to entertain them. Then the bride would appear. She was carried by her father or brother to the sedan chair. Then, when

A wedding procession. The sedan chair, carrying the bride, was carried by eight men.

the bride sat down in it, she would be taken to the bridegroom's house, together with the bridegroom and others. Upon arriving, the curtain of the sedan would be lifted and the bride would step out. But before this, a saddle would be laid in front of the sedan chair. When the bride came out of her sedan chair, she would have to cross the saddle first. This would assure that the bride would have a peaceful future. If the place where the new couple were to live was a two-room suite, the outer room would serve as the place for the wedding ceremony while the inner one would be the bedroom. A table would be laid out in the outer room and a man would be asked to light some joss-sticks to be placed in a pot sitting on the table. The bride and the bridegroom would kowtow to Heaven and Earth in front of this table. Then they would go into their bedroom and sit on the edge of the bed. Only then would the bridegroom lift the square cloth covering the head of the bride. Together, they would eat some "Offspring Bun" so as to assure that they would have many children; toast each other and prepare to go to bed.

A long wedding procession.

There would be more rituals after that, but I'd rather not to go into details. Early next morning, the bridegroom would announce that the girl was a virgin. A servant would then be sent to the bride's parents to announce this good news. At the moment of daybreak, a loud voice would

A newly wedded couple sit in their own room. The next item of the "procedures" would be lifting the cover off the head of the bride.

be heard in the alley leading to the house of the bride's parents crying "Good tidings!" Thus not only the girl's parents but also all neighbors would learn that the girl was a virgin. This was something of a great honor in those days. Alternately, a colored rosette would be hung in front of the gate of the bridegroom's house. It was a sign to indicate that the bride was a virgin. If people sent by the parents of the bride to bring the girl back home noticed that there was no such rosette at the gate, they would not have the courage to enter.

This shows that a happy event might not end in happiness. A consummation could only be made at the end of such an event.

As for funerals, there was great difference between those of the Hans and the Manchurians. Before the Republic, funeral procedures were extremely complicated. A funeral could easily exhaust people. Funerals for people like Ci Xi, Guang Xu, Yuan

An "attendant" of a wedding procession also functioned as a lamp holder.

When a person in a rich family died, a paper-made car would be brought to take that person to the nether world.

There was a Carrying House in old Beijing that specialized in carrying coffins for customers. Besides this, it provided all-round services for the family of the deceased. It was known throughout the country for its good service.

Shikai, Feng Guozhang and Jiang Guiti were most pompous. Take what people wore in funeral processions for instance. Such processions were simply fashion displays. Officers all wore ceremonial uniforms, officials in their Western suits with high hats. Officials of the former Qing Court put on their official robes. There were all sorts of paper-made replicas of various objects that would be used to accompany the deceased. These included replicas of boys, maids, houses, gardens, furniture, and even, sometimes, a motor car, as shown in the photo. Apparently, even in the nether world, the deceased would never forget how to enjoy the consumer goods of the West.

Like all Chinese, Beijingers attached great importance to the lunar New Year. They began to celebrate it in the mid 12th month of the lunar calendar and continued through to the 15th of the first month. Rich or poor, everyone hoped to have a peaceful New Year.

Three Festivals in the Capital

During the lunar New Year, women played mahjong to while away their time.

As time went by, society went through profound changes in all its aspects. But one thing remained unchanged - the attention given to the celebration of traditional festivals by Beijingers. China has been an agrarian country since ancient times and its festivals are mostly connected with farming. For example, the three greatest festivals all have something to do with the harvest, namely, the Spring Festival (lunar New Year), Dragon Boat Festival and Mid-autumn Festival. The Spring Festival is the most important of these.

In the old days, after a year's toil, peasants needed a break. Besides, it was so cold outside there was nothing one could do in the fields. So the peasants might sit on their brick beds and enjoy themselves at the time they set aside for relaxation at the end of the year. City folks also needed a rest after a year's hard work no matter what trade they might be engaged in. Those who made a bit of money would need to go over their accounting books. Those in debt would have to go

A hotpot was a must for the dinner of the New Year's Eve. Its steam added much to the New Year's festive atmosphere.

into hiding to avoid the lenders. If they could manage to do so on this occasion they might delay payment a bit longer.

When the New Year's Eve came, what was most important to everyone was a family reunion. If anyone was not home yet, all the other family members would wait together for him to come home. Only then would the dinner of the New Year's Eve start. This would be the most important dinner of the whole year and the food would be rich in variety and ample in quantity. After the dinner, the whole family would "keep vigil". People enjoyed themselves by chatting, eating sunflower seeds, making dumplings, playing cards, etc., waiting for the arrival of the New Year at midnight. At that moment, the whole city of Beijing would seem to boil over. Children would rush into the courtyards to light firecrackers. The big noise of bangs could be heard here and there and the air would be pungent with the

During the Chinese New Year, people, both old and young, enjoyed themselves by pasting paintings of Door Warriors on their gates, lighting fireworks and setting off firecrackers.

smell of gunpowder. In those days, firecrackers could only shoot about three meters high, so they could not illuminate the night sky. Educated people would come out at that moment to paste antithetical couplets on their gates. The ink on the scrolls might still be wet. The gates at that time were usually made of two boards, so the couplets would be pasted one on each board.

On the following day, the whole family clan would gather together to offer sacrifices to their ancestors. On a table would be spread ancestral wooden tablets, candles, dry and fresh fruit, and cakes. The members

The lunar New Year was the happiest moment for children.

On the first day of the first month of the lunar calendar, every family would hold a ceremony of sacrificing to their ancestors.

To paint a face, to wield a big knife, what a joy!

of the clan, in the order of their seniority, would kowtow to those tablets. After that, the younger generations would kowtow to the older generations. It was a most happy time for children because after each kowtow they would be given some money as the New Year's gift. With the money in their pockets, they could buy whatever they liked at the temple fair that would take place after the ceremony was over, and even their parents could not stop them from buying this or that. After all they were the owners of the money.

Starting from the second day of the New Year, relatives would begin visiting one another. The younger ones would go and see their elderly relatives. They would not go empty-handed. At the very least they would bring a box of cakes and cookies as a gift. Such visits could be exhausting. When relatives met, they would bow or kowtow to one another according to certain rules. Besides, they needed to exchange stereotyped greetings that sounded warm and amicable.

When everyone was tired of speaking, eating, visiting, etc., all needed a rest. The best way to do this would be to go to a theater. Beijing was full of good Peking opera performers. On the occasion of the New Year, the performers did not rest, for it was a good opportunity to earn money. The operas to be staged were usually amusing and ended in happiness. This was no time for tragedy, nor performances full of action that would be too tiring. It was a rest for audiences as well as for the actors. As long as they could make the audience happy, they did their job and would earn a good sum. The New Year festival in the old days was a big event. People began preparation a fortnight before the festival. After the New Year, they longed for the Lantern Festival (Yuan Xiao), which falls on the fifteenth day of the first lunar month. Only when *Yuan Xiao* was over, did the enthusiasm for the New Year celebration begin to peter out.

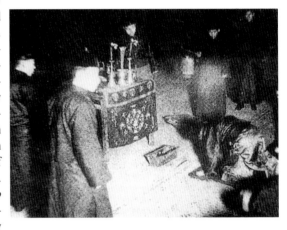

People of old Beijing kowtowed to usher in the God of Wealth on the eve of the lunar New Year. Despite their piety, the God of Wealth would never show up and most Beijingers lived in poverty.

The second most important festival was the Dragon Boat Festival. It was established to commemorate a great patriotic poet, Qu Yuan, of the Warring States Period. On such an occasion, *zongzi* is a must. In Beijing, unlike the southern parts of the country where glutinous rice of *zongzi* is often mixed with meat or bean paste, people like to mix dates in the *zongzi*. Another difference between the two areas is that people prefer to eat cold *zongzi* in Beijing whereas *zongzi* is eaten hot in the South. This festival in Beijing, however, was not celebrated as enthusiastically as it was in the South. First, Hunan where Qu Yuan had killed himself was a bit too far from Beijing. Second, Qu Yuan had been an intellectual who devoted all of himself to State affairs and the people of that time, which could not be fully understood by the folks in Beijing.

The third festival was the Mid-autumn Festival in August. The moon on that day was round and bright, cascading light onto the earth. A month before this festival in old Beijing, there were clay figurines called "Lord Rabbit" available for sale in all the streets. The rabbit had a human face and a rabbit's mouth, as well as two large rabbit ears. It was usually made in a seated posture, and dressed in a red robe with gold or silver decorative objects. It was said that Lord Rabbit placed in a shrine for worship at home would bring longevity to the worshiper. Lord Rabbit was of course a male. So a spouse was arranged for him by some people, hence the availability of Madame Rabbit.

Gongs and drums were beaten to celebrate the arrival of a new year on the first day of the first month.

As the Mid-autumn Festival approached, moon cakes appeared in the market in large quantity. The best-known ones were *zilaihong* and *zilaibai*, which were of good quality and inexpensive. At that time, the moon cakes of Guangdong style had not yet entered Beijing. It was a harvest season festival and fruit such as pears, dates, apples, etc. filled the market. So under a bright

Fascinating lamps of all kinds in the market.

moon, a family would sit in the courtyard around a table laid with such fruit and enjoy themselves. Young men and women of eligible age for marriage would look at the moon and make wishes on the sly, hoping to have a happy family of their own in the future.

One noticeable feature of the three traditional festivals is that most people changed their usual activities and experienced new roles during the festivals. They would become thoroughly engulfed in an atmosphere of legends and traditional culture. Children and women in particular would have such feelings. In return, they would affect men or even the head of a clan. Why is it that it was men who were the last to be moved by the festival atmosphere? Because this was time that they had to repay all their debts. That weighed on their minds. In those days, customers were allowed to pay a grocery bill all at once on festival days, for what they had bought in the past. This probably had something to do with the nature of agrarian society in China. Didn't the peasants first work hard for a year and then get the harvest all at once later?

An old man selling clay figurines of Lord Rabbit.

A man playing a flute in the courtyard of quiet *siheyuan*. What was he telling us? Probably of his loneliness and boredom with life.

Awning, Fish Pot and Pomegranates, Chef, Fat Dog and Plump Girl

Here I would like to describe to you some very brief scenes often seen in a *siheyuan*.

Spring pancakes: As a rule, the spring pancakes were served on the beginning day of spring every year. One might have them in a restaurant or at home. They might be served at a grand dinner or taken as a casual meal. The dough was mixed with hot water and a little sesame oil kneaded in. This was then made into thin pancakes and steamed. Each pancake was then used to wrap up some cooked meat and uncooked greens, which were dipped in bean paste. The cooked meat was shreds of braised meat from the upper part of a leg of pork, shredded tripe, shredded roast chicken, shreds of stewed duck meat, shreds of seasoned meat, shredded donkey meat, or shreds of some other type of meat. To go with the meat were panned bean sprouts mixed with vermicelli, stir-fried spinach, stir-fried chives, stir-fried lily flowers and fungi, scrambled eggs, etc. Everyone made his or her own combination with a mixture of the above dishes. The whole family sat around a table and busily made such bundles with the spring pancakes and ate heartily. The festive atmosphere on such occasions was most important to everyone. When I was small, spring pancakes were a must on this festival day. I did eat them occasionally at other times, but then the atmosphere was not so festive.

When a person had some money in Beijing, what

An elderly man of old Beijing.

should he do with it? The best plan was probably to buy a house. No matter how chaotic society might be, a house could always be leased and the rent was assured. Of all houses, a *siheyuan* would be the best. One criterion for an ideal *siheyuan* in Beijing was that it must have an awning, fish pots, a pomegranate tree,

Doing homework after school in a courtyard.

a chef, a fat dog and plump girls.

Taking a bath: Elderly people in the area of Jiangsu and Zhejiang had the habit of drinking tea in the morning and having a bath in the evening. In the old days in Beijing, a person would go to a public bath house to get thoroughly cleaned. Renowned actors of Peking opera were quite fond of taking their baths at the public bath house, though they all had bath facilities at home. Ma Lianliang, for example, made it a habit to take

Descendants of Prince Gong of the late Qing dynasty in their own residence.

a bath at Huaqing Pool in the afternoon before he was going to give a performance that evening. What is more, he preferred to take his bath in a pool with the hottest water. As he was about to end his bath, he would shout a few times to see if his voice was in good register. An attendant would then go to the Dong Lai Shun Restaurant, across the street, to bring some food over for him. Li Shaochun, another famous actor, was also fond of taking baths in a public bath house. If he happened to meet some of his fans there, half a day would easily be spent in the bath.

Enjoying roast meat: In the beginning, eating roast meat was a privilege for men. The best restaurants that

Lady with bound feet and her maid-in-waiting enjoying the sunshine. This photo was taken some 80 years ago.

provided roast meat were three, namely, the Roast Meat Garden (*Kaorou Wan*), the Roast Meat Ji (*Kaorou Ji*) and the Roast Meat Wang (*Kaorou Wang*). The method of roasting meat was this: usually there was a large table with a big hole in the center where one could see burning charcoal in a stove. Over this stove was some kind of an iron grill made of thick iron bars. Eaters sitting around the table would put slices of meat on to the hot iron grill to roast it. While drinking alcohol, they heartily ate the roast meat. The simmering meat dripped grease into the fire, which often leapt up emitting fragrance. The Roast Meat Garden was the first to be established. The meat it sold was true veal. The Roast Meat Ji opened a little later. Because of its good location by Lake Houhai, its business was brisk. Even in the heat of summer, the heat for meat roasting was quite bearable because the tall willow trees by the lake provided coolness. Besides, this meat was served together with lotus leave congee and ox-tongue-shaped pancakes. This restaurant was a strong competitor of the Roast Meat Garden.

While men were busy outside, women managed the home.

Drinking liquor from a vat: In the liquor shops for the lower classes, there was no table but a vat of liquor bedded halfway in the ground. The part sticking out of the ground served as a table. There was little food to go with the liquor. It was, however, a place for those who could afford the time to chat as they drank..

Small eateries: When a few friends were gathered at someone's home for a chat, the host might take them to a nearby eatery when the time came for a meal. Since both the owner and the waiters were probably familiar with this customer, he did not have to do the ordering. They knew what he would want and just brought the food to his table. If a gourmet came for a visit, the

Enjoying meat soup and a pancake.

eatery would ask him to prepare one or two recipes. The gourmet would then tell the waiter what ingredients to use, how to use the chopper, the sequence in which the ingredients were to be put into the cauldron, how long they should be cooked, etc. The chef would listen carefully behind a curtain of the kitchen. When the dish was ready to serve, the chef would come to the table too. The gourmet, the owner and the chef would discuss how the food tasted. Perhaps this would become one of the special dishes for this eatery in future.

Many renowned gourmets went to restaurants familiar to them. If a gourmet was going to throw a party, it would be best to go to one of those restaurants. After the meal, he might say to the owner, "Bill, please!" The owner would reply readily, "Okay! Thanks a lot!" But he needed not to pay right away. Bills were collected from such gourmets three times a year, usually before the Spring Festival, the Dragon Boat Festival and the Mid-Autumn Festival. A well-dressed waiter would call on those gourmets to collect the money. The records of each payment owed to the restaurant was clearly written. A gourmet would not bother to peruse those records, because he would not remember clearly how many times he had visited the restaurant. As long as he had the money, he would make the payment readily. Was this method beneficial to the restaurant or the gourmet? Maybe it was beneficial to both.

Mutton: The best place for buying mutton was Yue Sheng Zhai, where they boasted that their stewing gravy had been kept cooking for over a hundred years. The taste of their mutton was certainly unique. Most people preferred to eat mutton in summer. A customer would usually carry a little pot in which to place the mutton they bought in this store. When a man entered, a waiter who might know him would cry, "What kind of mutton would you like to have today, sir? Braised or stewed?" All the customer needed to do was to shoot a glance at the stewed mutton and tell the attendant the amount he needed. When the attendant weighed a chunk of mutton, the customer would shove his little pot over the counter. The attendant would take the pot

Pancakes were roasted and would be hung high until they were ready to be served.

Woman having her breakfast in a street of old Beijing.

A chef of Shandong cuisine.

and turn to a large barrel, lift its lid and ladle some gravy into the pot. Then he would put the stewed mutton into the pot and say, "Here you are, sir." As the customer turned to leave, the attendant would immediately call out, "Good bye!"

The culture of Beijing and past events in Beijing cannot all be contained in one book. It would be impossible to cover all aspects of the secular life of Beijingers, or all aspects of life in the imperial house. Many of these are now forgotten; many have become topics of conversation for leisure time. Many we might speak of in the future.

Editors' Note

Changes a city has undergone are an important part of the history of the development of a civilization. In publishing this series of books, we have been guided by one consideration, i.e., to give readers a brief history of some well-known Chinese cities by looking at some old sepia photos taken there and reading some remembrances with regard to those cities.

Not like conventional publications, each book of this series contains a large number of old photos selected to form a pictorial commentary on the text. This provides a good possibility for readers to learn about Chinese urban history, cultural evolution in urban society in a new perspective. It also enables readers to re-experience historical "vicissitudes" of those cities and relish feelings of urban folks of China in the modern times.

To better illustrate those cities, we have commissioned renowned writers who have not only lived in their respective cities for a long time but also have been known for their strong local writing style. Either in presenting a panoramic view of a city or depicting fate of men in street, their writings are always so natural yet full of feelings.

This series of books have been published originally in Chinese by Jiangsu Fine Art Publishing House. The English edition has been published jointly by the Foreign Languages Press and Jiangsu Fine Art Publishing House.

Foreign Languages Press
Oct.2000 Beijing

图书在版编目(CIP)数据

老北京:帝都遗韵:英文/徐城北著. —北京:外文出版社,2001
(老城市系列)
ISBN 7-119-02786-7

Ⅰ.老… Ⅱ.徐… Ⅲ.北京市-地方史-史料-英文 Ⅳ.K291
中国版本图书馆 CIP 数据核字(2000)第 78795 号

中文原版

选题策划	叶兆言　何兆兴　顾华明　速加
主　　编	朱成梁
副 主 编	何兆兴　吕平
著　　文	徐城北
图片供稿	中国照片档案馆　中国第二历史档案馆　张洪杰
装帧设计	顾华明
责任编辑	何兆兴

英文版

策划编辑	兰佩瑾
翻　　译	王明杰
英文编辑	卓柯达
责任编辑	孙树明

老北京·帝都遗韵

ⓒ外文出版社

外文出版社出版
(中国北京百万庄大街24号)
邮政编码 100037
外文出版社网址:http://www.flp.com.cn
外文出版社电子信箱:info@flp.com.cn
　　　　　　　　　sales@flp.com.cn
利丰雅高制作(深圳)有限公司印刷
2001年(大32开)第1版
2001年第1版第1次印刷
(英文)
ISBN 7-119-02786-7/J·1553(外)
08000(精)

OLD CITY